Organizing for Work

Henry Laurence Gantt

Edited with introduction by

Donald A. Forrer

Published by Donald A. Forrer - 2006

Organizing for Work

Henry Laurence Gantt

Edited with Introduction by

Donald A. Forrer

Introduction Copyright 2006
by Donald A. Forrer

"Organizing for Work" Copyright 1919
By
Harcourt, Brace and Howe, Inc.

Books may be ordered through booksellers or by contacting:

Dr. Donald A. Forrer
dforrer@swfla.rr.com
http://www.professorforrer.com

ISBN: 0-9779157-0-0
ISBN13: 978-0-9779157-0-5

Printed in the United States of America

Acknowledgements

Special Thanks to:

Dr. Joseph Heinzman Jr., Mrs. Sandy Heinzman, Ms. Marilyn Benson
& especially my wife, Janet.

The editing assistance and content clarification provided throughout
this process was greatly appreciated.

The cover of this publication was created by

Orlando Artist; Ms. Zila Forrer.

Zila Forrer is a Latin artist specializing in idealized realism. Born in Aguadilla, Puerto Rico, Zila obtained her Bachelors of Fine Art at the University of Central Florida. Zila works as an art teacher and her art has been featured and presented at art exhibitions throughout Florida. Her art has been displayed in newspapers (La Prensa, Orlando Sentinel, etc.) and art magazines alike (Open House of Arts). She has also conducted a drawing seminar in a prestigious International Association.

Zila's purpose is to unveil the beauty of God's creation in a new and different way, learning to appreciate the inner beauty that many of us take for granted. Her work expresses the eloquence found in objects, animals, and the human figure. Her art captures not only the physical aspects of the subject, but also the emotional and spiritual beauty that is often difficult to see. Her work has been said to embody "A life long quest to find truth, not just of oneself, but also of the world that surrounds us." (Ryan Allen May)

View Zila's art at:

http://www.zilagallery.com/

About the Author

Donald A. Forrer, D.B.A.

Don Forrer has a Doctorate in Business Administration and serves as the Director of the MBA/MPA program at International College of Naples, Florida. He served as a management professor at Troy State University, Strayer University, Embry-Riddle University, & International College. He has lectured on management topics in Taiwan, Japan, Guam, and throughout the United States. Don has presented his research at prestigious international conferences, including the Heathcare Technology Management Association in Warwick, England and the Production and Operations Management Society at Chicago, San Francisco, Orlando, & Savannah. Don was the Operations Director at Troy State University & Director of Information and Management for the city of Cape Coral, Florida, where he managed the revenues and information technology during a conversion from a flat file system to a relational database system. After a 20 year career with the U.S. Army, Don retired in 1992. During his last four years with the army, he managed the official authorizations database, as the army downsized from 750,000 personnel to 520,000 personnel. Don currently provides consulting for small businesses and provides workshops for new businesses in southwest Florida. Additionally, he writes a weekly business column for the Naples Daily News and the Cape Coral Daily Breeze and is published in other notable newspapers throughout the United States.

Table of Contents

Introduction
By Donald A. Forrer

This introduction accompanies a reprinted book entitled "Organizing for Work" written by Henry Laurence Gantt in 1919. The introduction explores how Gantt, and, to a lesser extent, Frederick Taylor and other theorists, management style and principles are accepted in today's business environment. Additionally, this research examines the evolution of management thought over the past century, explores management practices, and considers what works versus what does not.

Could Henry Gantt, Frederick Taylor, Henri Fayol, and other theorists of their era function in today's environment? Are the theories and practices of these early theorists still applicable? In academia, scientific managers are considered management pioneers. Modern management theories and practices evolved from their principles and writings. Exactly how affluent early theorists were to the formulation of today's management principles is an interesting question. One purpose of this introduction is to address this elusive topic.

As theorists analyzed management throughout the years, several models were developed to deal with the complex world of managing people. Frederick Taylor wrote the following about the importance of interaction between management and employees.[8]

> Page 35 - 36: "And this presents a very simple though effective illustration of what in meant by the words "prosperity for the employee, coupled with prosperity for the employer", the two principle objects of management".

Henry Gantt and Frederick Taylor spent much time developing and evaluating principles of management, time studies, and charts. The underlying concept of their research was that profits should be fairly distributed among workers and employers, with employees receiving fair wages for completed work. It is likely that both would be

1

disappointed in the scandalous management behavior at Tyco, Enron, and WorldCom.

During the years since Gantt and Taylor pioneered scientific management theories, there have been many examples of executive greed and union issues that stress the relationship between management and employees. Theorists analyze numerous aspects of leadership, motivation, and behavior to determine what makes the perfect organization. It is my contention that this process began with early theorists and the influence of Taylor and Gantt is still present today.

Gantt's management theories were certainly not considered or practiced by greedy executives during the scandal at Enron. During one year, the top five Enron executives drew $282.7 million in compensation, while employees were urged to invest in the company. When Enron financially unraveled, executives received millions of dollars in stock options, while employees lost most of their investments. These hard working employees were not rewarded with fair compensation as Gantt advocated.[1]

Gantt and Taylor believed good employees were valuable assets and should be paid for production and protected by management. Imagine their concern if they read headlines reporting that Ford cutting 30,000 employees and General Motors eliminating 35,000 jobs.[2] It is highly possible they would feel both management and labor could do more to preclude this from occurring.

Gantt believed that management should rely on measurement and forecasting to protect the health of the company. Industry analysts blame Ford and General Motors (GM) with poor planning for a global market, resulting in layoffs and plant closings. Since 1993, General Motors has reduced their workforce by 50%, closing eight plants and eliminating 127,000 jobs.[2] Even though many economists blame foreign competition and plants moving overseas, Toyota operates 12 plants and employs 37,000 in the United States (U.S.), while Honda has three plants in the U.S., with 25,000 U.S. employees.[3] It could be that management as well as competition deserves the blame.

Neither Gantt nor Taylor considered executive or employee greed when they conducted their research to look for the "one best way" for employee production. It was a vastly different business environment in their era. With Internet access, they could have known how the directors of The Boston Pacific Railroad defrauded the government in 1872. The Boston Pacific Railroad managed a publicly traded company, while also owning the company that was assigned most of the work.[4] Many may argue that executives who lead their company to huge profits deserve to benefit. Unfortunately, in numerous cases, executives prosper, while their companies suffer.

Based on research, Gantt and Taylor never considered executive compensation as an issue. However, excessive compensation practices for senior executives did not begin with the CEO and CFO of Tyco. They rewarded themselves $466 million over a three year period, which contributed to financial problems for their company. Nor did excessive compensation practices for senior executives begin when the Chairman of WorldCom was awarded a severance package which included $1.5 million per annum for life.[5] In fact, the president of Bethlehem Steel earned $1.6 million as a bonus in 1929.[4]

Many consider Taylor, Gantt, Fayol, et. al., production oriented managers who believed employees were expendable and not important to the equation. However, it is probable they provided future behavioral theorists with a foundation for behavioral theory. In truth, this group of scientific managers demonstrated through their research they cared about workers willing to work for fair wages. They also consistently demonstrated they had limited tolerance for employees who did not meet reasonable productivity goals.

Gantt and Taylor did not have to consider employee abuse as an issue in the early 1900's. In today's management world, we contend with unions, attorneys, and government regulations designed to ensure that workers are not abused. Employee abuse preventatives are necessary, but have evolved since inception. These same abuse preventatives now contribute to non-productivity by some employees who abuse the very system designed to protect them. Laws and regulations designed to ensure fairness are manipulated by some workers abusing the system; resulting in decreased company revenue and contributing to jobs lost to other countries with less stringent regulations and less government oversight. Ultimately, this is not beneficial for the American worker.

This reference to today's business environment is not to imply that modern laws and regulations to protect employees are not necessary. Nor is this statement designed to be construed as union or attorney bashing. This conclusion is merely an attempt to apply common sense to necessary laws and procedures that should provide America with improved workplaces. It is unacceptable to use a system which allows greedy union officials and attorneys to exploit language in contracts and legislation to make a few people wealthy, while jeopardizing the majority's livelihood. Early theorists researching management practices to improve conditions and compensation for employees did not foresee these management/employee developments.

The following segment of this introduction provides a short history of management thought. It is not meant to be inclusive, but to provide a modern applicable management thought platform for the 1919 Henry Laurence Gantt book "Organizing for Work".[6]

Management Thought

Management thought evolved, over many years, as theorists and managers worked to improve conditions in the workplace. Early theorists played key roles in establishing accepted management practices and principles. This introduction examines Gantt's ideas and practices while providing a brief study of other key management theorists.

It is my contention that this introduction outlines the influence of early theorists on the evolution of management thought. Each era of management builds on the past and continues to examine critical issues in the workplace. Management thought did not begin with Frederick Taylor, Max Weber, Henri Fayol, and Henry Gantt. Earlier influences by Machiavelli, Sun Tzu, and others helped form management practices and principles that could easily be adapted today.

Theorists and managers have worked together to improve efficiency and effectiveness for hundreds of years. For the purpose of this introduction, we will begin with the scientific management era. *Figure 1* portrays the introduction authors' sample of core contributors to management thought. Significant eras are subdivided for clarity.

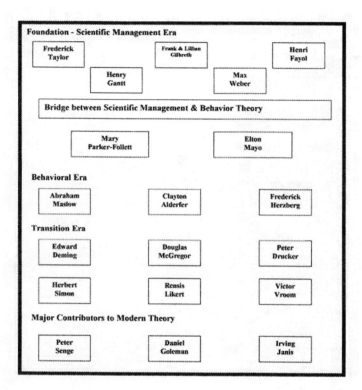

Figure 1 – *A chart of prominent management theorists. This chart is not inclusive, but designed to introduce key players in the formation of current management thought.*

The theorists listed in *figure1* illustrate significant contributors to the evolution of management thought. The theorists in *figure 1* serve as a starting point for those who want to study the development of major theories in management. Research conducted by theorists listed below contributed significantly and formed the foundation of modern principles and practices. *Figure 2* provides the timeframe for each of the theorists that we discuss in this introduction.

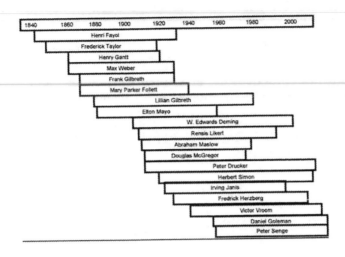

Figure 2 – *Timeline*
Contributed by Dr. Joseph Heinzman – used with permission.

Scientific Management Era (1881-1923)

Scientific Management was primarily developed to increase productivity in the industrialized world. In 1800, 90% of the United State's population relied on agriculture for subsistence.[7] By 1900, this reliance was significantly reduced to 33%.[7] This shift of socio-cultural orientation from agriculture to industrialization created a need for a management structure that could transition the masses into industrial work. To understand how many of the models were derived, it is important to discuss the contributions of early theorists. These theorists were responsible for shaping the direction of management thought and their influence is evident in many of our modern management models. Early management was influenced by scientific thinkers such as Frederick Taylor, Max Weber, and Henri Fayol. Scientific management was necessary due to the need for increased productivity and effective methods to manage workers.

Contributions of early scientific management included the assembly line. The assembly line modernized production facilities and greatly improved productivity. The concept of scientific management caused anxiety among workers because they feared increased productivity would cause personnel layoffs or work shortages. Unfortunately, the strict practices of early scientific management encouraged some managers to abuse workers.[8] This employee abuse caused unanticipated problems in the workforce, promoted the need for Unions and employee protection laws, and led to many of the future studies outlined in this introduction.

"Organizing for Work" was written during the *"Classical School"* period of management (1900 to 1920). This school of management thought concentrated on increased productivity and managing the individual worker. The *"Classical School"*, period developed to meet the challenges of managing complex organizations such as factories.[9]

During this period, managers concentrated on efficiency and were primarily practitioners. Most early theorists managed plants and dealt on a daily basis with the management issues being studied. Scientific management focuses on the "one best way" to accomplish a task, consequently improving effectiveness through efficiency. The goal was to improve production, raise wages for the worker, and reduce costs for the company.

Frederick Taylor (1856-1915) is widely acclaimed as the *"Father of Scientific Management"*. He based his writings on research conducted at three different steel mills. His most acclaimed research, the *"Pig Iron Studies"*, concentrated on increased efficiency and increased pay for the workers. Taylor's model is credited for large increases in productivity with fewer workers and in less time. According to Wrege and Perroni, Frederick Taylor's account of loading pig-iron has been accepted throughout the management world.[10]

Even though Taylor was born to an affluent family, he worked his way through the employee ranks at Midvale Steel. From 1878 to 1884, Taylor worked as a laborer and was eventually promoted to chief engineer.[7] Taylor's promotion progression through the ranks afforded him the perspective of a laborer and the insight of management.

Taylor believed it was necessary to increase the efficiency of workers to expand productivity. Taylor's ideas grew primarily from his years of experience and experiments with three companies: Midvale Steel, Simonds Rolling Machine, and Bethlehem Steel.

Taylor consistently applied the following questions:

1. Was there one best way of doing things?
2. Could some elements of work be eliminated or parts of the operation combined?
3. Could the sequences of the processes be improved?

Beginning in 1881, Taylor utilized production line time studies to support his managerial system.[11] He believed a total mental revolution had to take place in order to increase productivity. His theory stressed that management and labor should understand they both had a common interest in the productivity of the plant. Taylor's philosophy came from four principles:

1. Develop a science for each employee's work

2. Scientifically select the most qualified person for the job and train them in the procedures they are expected to follow
3. Cooperate with employees to ensure work is performed the prescribed way
4. Division of work to ensure planning, organizing, and controlling are the prime responsibility of management rather than the individual worker

During June of 1976, Peter Drucker[12] wrote that Frederick Taylor determined four major changes must occur in an organization to increase productivity. These changes were:

1. Higher wages
2. Elimination of physical strain and bodily damage caused from performing work requirements incorrectly
3. Utilization of scientific management to develop human personality to its fullest
4. Utilization of scientific management to eliminate the boss

Total Quality Management (TQM) has similarities to Taylor's management theories. Taylor's research concentrated on improving efficiency, finding it extremely difficult while working with management attitudes of the early 1900's. Efficiency is one of the most difficult areas of business to improve because management has to review workers and consider how they accomplish their daily functions. This is usually unpopular with employees and becomes less popular when management attempts to improve employee efficiency.

Over 100 years ago, Frederick Taylor addressed this issue and improved efficiency by 300%, while reducing personnel requirements by half. However, he noted it took strong leadership and support from his board, due to the political pressure placed on him by his employees. This aspect of management has not changed since 1901.

Henry Gantt (1861-1919) worked with Frederick Taylor at all three steel plants and, as a consultant, revisited Taylor's incentive plans. Gantt devised a chart that is still used to determine worker productivity. In his methodology, workers were tracked daily; using a black bar if they made their quota and a red bar if they were unsuccessful. This chart evolved over the years and is known as a *"Gantt Chart"*.[13]

Henry Gantt developed the *Gantt Chart* in 1911 and perfected it during the First World War.[7] Gantt utilized the efficiency of measurement to improve productivity. Additionally, Gantt focused on motivation associated with rewards for positive productivity rather than concentrate on punishment associated with negative productivity. He is credited for developing a wage system that guaranteed the worker a minimum wage. This wage system allowed bonuses for workers who met or exceeded goals. Gantt's research also concentrated on leadership skills necessary to be successful in an industrial setting.[13]

The GANTT chart, also known as the waterfall chart, is used in today's business to track a variety of activities including action items and project and production activities. These tasks are connected in detail precedence diagram networks to determine interdependencies and the critical path. The GANTT chart was the foundation of modern planning and scheduling systems.[14]

Frank (1868-1924) and Lillian Gilbreth (1878-1972)

focused on motion studies. Their belief that work design would allow operational time to be determined in advance was very effective by breaking work down to sub elements and improving efficiency. The Gilbreth's theory is easily associated with Total Quality Management, a theory introduced over a half century later. They broke "work" down to its lowest component, studied it individually, and applied how work affects the entire organization. Once analyzed, the best method to reduce waste was devised and studied.[8]

The Gilbreth's most recognized study involved bricklayers. Frank worked as an apprentice bricklayer. Starting at the age of 17, Frank was eventually promoted to chief superintendent at Whiden Company.[7] By studying motion, Frank designed scaffolding that eliminated bending and unnecessary movement which doubled productivity. However, most union workers refused to adapt Gilbreth's methodology, which kept the practice of old fatiguing methods in place.

Frank noticed three different motions used by bricklayers:

1. One for teaching
2. One for working fast
3. One for slowing the pace of the work

After careful study, Frank devised a series of motions that tripled the amount of work that a bricklayer could accomplish in a day. His technique used a motion picture camera to observe work and then determined the most economical method of accomplishing the work. Frank and Lillian argued that motion studies would increase productivity and employee morale because it demonstrated that management was concerned about employees.[15]

Taylor wrote this about Frank Gilbreth:[8]

> Page 59: "And the reader, by calling to mind the gain which was made by Mr. Gilbreth through his motion and time study in laying bricks, will appreciate the great possibilities for quicker methods of doing all kinds of hand work which lie in every tradesman after he has the help which comes from a scientific motion and time study of his work".

> Page 61: "Even the motion study of Mr. Gilbreth in bricklaying involves a much more elaborate

investigation than that which occurs in most cases. The general steps to be taken in developing a simple law of this class are as follows".

"First: Find, say, 10 to 15 different men (preferably in as many separate establishments and different parts of the country) who are especially skillful in doing the particular work to be analyzed".

"Second: Study the exact series of elementary operations or motions which each of these men uses in doing the work which is being investigated, as well as the implements each man uses".

"Third: Study with a stop-watch the time required to make each of these elementary movements and then select the quickest way of doing each element of the work".

"Fourth: Eliminate all false movements, slow movements, and useless movements".

"Fifth: After doing away with all unnecessary movements, collect into one series the quickest and best movements as well as the best implements. This doing away with all unnecessary movements, collect into one series the quickest and best movements as well as the best implements".

Frank and Lillian Gilbreth, as a husband and wife team, influenced scientific management by including human elements in their research. Lillian's dissertation appeared in the book *"Psychology of Management"* after it was first published in the Industrial Engineering Magazine in 1912. Written during an era when women theorists were not recognized or accepted, Lillian insisted that the publication list her as L.M. Gilbreth, thus, hiding the fact she was female. She and Frank worked together on fatigue and motion studies. However, Lillian also focused on how the human element was promoted. She believed that scientific management had one main objective; to help workers obtain their potential as human beings.[15]

Taylor wrote:[8]

Page 38 – 39: "Mr. Frank B. Gilbreth, a member of our Society, who had himself studied bricklaying in his youth, became interested in the principles of scientific management, and decided to apply them to the art of bricklaying. He made an intensely interesting analysis and study of each movement of the bricklayer, and one after another eliminated all unnecessary movements and substituted fast for slow motions. He experimented with every minute element which in any way affects the speed and the tiring of the bricklayer". "He developed the exact position which each of the feet of the bricklayer should occupy with relation to the wall, the mortar box, and the pile of bricks, and so made it necessary for him to take a step or two toward the pile of bricks and back again each time a brick is laid".

Page 39 - 40: Through all of this minute study of motions to be made by the bricklayer in laying bricks under standard conditions, Mr. Gilbreth has reduced his movements from eighteen motions per brick to five, and even in one case to as low as two motions per brick. He has given all of the details of this analysis to the profession in the chapter headed "Motion Study" of his book entitled "Bricklaying System", published by Myron C. Clerk Publishing Company, New York and Chicago; E. F. N. Spon, of London".

Page 42: "The management must also recognize the broad fact that workmen will not submit to this more rigid standardization and will not work extra hard, unless they receive extra pay for doing it".

Page 42 – 43: "The writer has gone fully into Mr. Gilbreth's method in order that it may be perfectly clear that this increase in output and that this harmony could not have been attained under the management of "initiative and incentive" (that is, by putting the problem up to the workman and leaving him to solve it alone) which has been the philosophy of the past. And that his success has been due to the use of the four elements which constitute the essence of scientific management".

"First: The development (by the management, not the workman) of the science of bricklaying, with rigid rules for each motion of every man, and the perfection and standardization of all implements and working conditions".

"Second: The careful selection and subsequent training of the bricklayers into first-class men, and the elimination of all men who refuse to or are unable to adopt the best method".

"Third: Bringing the first-class bricklayer and the science of bricklaying together, through the constant help and watchfulness of the management, and through paying each man a large daily bonus for working fast and doing what he is told to do".

"Fourth: An almost equal division of the work and responsibility between the workman and the management".

Together, Frank and Lillian Gilbreth developed a three-position plan to serve as an employee development program. According to this plan, a worker would first learn the job, then perform his or her job, and finally train others to do the job. Potentially, every employee was a learner, doer, and teacher for the organization. Employees looked forward to new opportunities and morale improved throughout the organization.

After Frank died in 1924, Lillian continued with their research until 1972 and became known as the *"First Lady of Management"*. This was partially due to her success in a man's world of management. Lillian also raised their 12 children, age two through nineteen.[7] The movie, *"Cheaper by the Dozen,"* was inspired by the Gilbreths. In 1935, Lillian became the first female professor of management at Newark College of Engineering.[7] Her work was the cornerstone of many management theories we still use today.[15]

Henri Fayol (1841-1925) desired to increase productivity in the individual worker and the workplace. Fayol felt good management principles could make any manager successful if applied properly.[16]

Fayol graduated from College in 1860. He worked his way through the ranks and was promoted to managing director in 1888 at the only company that he worked for, Commentry-Fourchambault Company.[7] Fayol wrote from the perspective of the Chief Executive Officer (CEO) and presented a paper on his management philosophy in 1900.[7]

Fayol divided the business operations into *six closely dependent activities*:

1. The **technical** aspects of producing and manufacturing products
2. The **commercial** aspects of buying raw materials and selling products
3. The **financial** aspects of acquiring and using capital
4. The **security** aspects of protecting employees and property
5. The **accounting** aspects of costs, profits, and liabilities
6. The **managerial** aspects

Fayol's focus was on managerial aspects, believing workers would follow if managers followed his guidelines.[16]

According to Fayol,[16] effective management can be defined in *five functions*:

1. **Planning** or devising a plan that will meet the organizations goals
2. **Organizing** or combining the human elements with resources to meet the organizations goals
3. **Commanding** or causing the human assets to work toward the organizations goals
4. **Coordinating** or ensuring the human assets and resources work together in harmony
5. **Controlling** or measuring and monitoring to ensure the goals of the organization are met

Fayol believed a manager's ability to manage is directly correlated to his/her position in the hierarchy. Lower level managerial positions required technical skills, but few management skills. As employees are promoted up the strategic hierarchy it becomes more important for them to have and utilize good management skills. As an owner of a business, it is imperative you select managers for their management skills, as well as their technical skills. If your business is small, it is important you manage your employees for success.

Fayol devised fourteen management principles (*table 1*) to ensure effective and efficient management.[16]

Fayol's Fourteen (14) Management Principles	
Division of labor	Remuneration
Stability of staff	Centralization
Authority	The hierarchy
Discipline	Order
Unity of command	Equity
Unity of direction	Initiative
Subordination of the individual	Esprit de corps

Table 1: *Fayol's fourteen management principles.*

Fayol chose the term "principles" rather than laws of management to separate them from the rigid concept of law. Fayol felt that a principle is hardly ever applied the same and managers' should have lead-way to insert his/her own personality into the application.[16]

Another early theorist, **Max Weber (1864-1920)**, is known as the *"Father of Organizational Theory"* and the *"Father of Bureaucracy"*.[7] Weber examined the type of management philosophy required to improve productivity and efficiency. Weber had a profound impact on how to expand productivity through good management and utilization of authority. It was Weber's conceptualization of bureaucracy that warranted the titles bestowed upon him by future theorists.[17]

Weber advocated three types of legitimate authority:[17]

1. Rational legal or the legal right of those elevated to authority
2. Traditional or a belief in the legitimacy of the traditional management principles coupled with the authority of those exercising authority
3. Charismatic or leadership based on the charisma of the individual in charge

Weber believed authority was the cornerstone of any organization. Weber's contributions to management thought were many, but his thoughts and research on organizational structure set standards for the future.[18] Weber's essential elements of organization included:

- A division of labor that clearly defined authority and responsibility
- A hierarchical structure resulting in a chain of command
- Technical qualifications utilized as a method of choosing employees
- The administrative official is not the owner of the organization being managed
- The administrator is subject to rules, regulations, and discipline.

The rules should be uniform
- Appointed officials, not elected
- Career officers that work for fixed wages

According to Max Weber, management should measure everything, hire good managers, provide leadership, and look for the best way to accomplish the task. The task is accomplished through strong leadership, willingness to make the difficult decisions, and the ability to guide employees to improvement. Improving efficiency can increase productivity and reduce personnel expenses.

Max Weber described modern public management in theory, but even he had his doubts about the opportunities for success of the model he created. Bendix quoted Weber as saying: "It is horrible to think that the world could one day be filled with nothing but those little cogs, little men clinging to little jobs and striving towards bigger ones".[19] His research resulted in a theory of organizational relationships and structures and described his version of an ideal organization called a bureaucracy. Weber's research resulted in his principles of management and, if adhered, would help any manager.

The first principle, *Division of Labor,* is used by managers to increase efficiency and output through specialization of labor. Providing junior managers with the *Authority* to make decisions and take action improves operations. For this critical element of leadership to succeed, managers must understand the organizations philosophy and accept the responsibility of making decisions for the company.

An extremely important principle, *Discipline*, dictates that all employees are loyal and obey the policies and procedures of the organization. The ability to discipline employees, not promoting the company's interests, is paramount to a leader's success. *Unity of Command* states that employees should serve only one boss and *Unity of Direction* states the company should have one plan or philosophy. If managers are constantly receiving an unclear message or reacting to double standards, it is extremely difficult to determine the course of action necessary for success.

Subordination of Individual Interests to the General Interest is a valuable principle for the organization. If employees are promoting their own agenda instead of the company philosophy, it will be obvious to customers and harm the company. An organization that has self-promoting employees concerned with building resumes will experience decreased productivity.

The process of paying employees a fair wage called *Remuneration* is the seventh principle. Employees expect and deserve the best pay a company can afford for their efforts. Another motivation principle is *Centralization of Decision Making.* Employees and managers should be involved with the decision making process if possible and appropriate. This does not mean that management should relinquish authority, but should consult surrounding experience. This action will result in better decisions and satisfied employees who feel that management values their experience.

The *Scalar Chain* indicates how decisions flow from senior management to the lowest point in the employee chain. An open line of communication is vital to productivity in a growing organization. The tenth principle, *Order,* is the assurance that people and materials are in the right place at the right time. This requires sound policies, enforced by management. More importantly, these policies must be institutionalized as the philosophy of the company. Customer service, a quality product, and employee relationships depend on it.

The ability of management to be fair to employees is *Equity.* As often noted by football coach and motivational speaker, Lou Holts, employees want to know the following three things about their leaders: 1) can they trust you, 2) do you care about them, and 3) do you know what you are talking about. If you achieve this through requirements, you will be viewed as equitable.

Employees work better for organizations that have *Stability of Tenure.* The true mark of a great organization is apparent when employee retention is high. This is a direct reflection on the leadership of the organization. The extent employees are allowed to demonstrate *Initiative,* is another test for the firm. The ability to make changes and operational flexibility will cause employees to exert a higher level of energy.

The last principle is certainly not the least important principle. The ability of senior leadership to establish *Esprit de Corps* in your organization is vital to success. Harmony and unity in the organization through team spirit will encourage employees to reflect positively on the firm, both at work and in the community after work.[18]

It is interesting that the studies of leaders such as Max Weber, Frederick Taylor, Henry Gantt and others conducted at the beginning of the twentieth century are still valid today. Terminologies have changed over the years, but most of the concepts have remained the same. However, if a company takes care of employees and customers, make a good quality product, and service their product, the company will be successful.

Therefore, the scientific management era concentrated on effectiveness and efficiency, but included employee concerns and work conditions. The economic times of the early 1900's allowed managers to discard employees who did not perform, while rewarding those willing to work efficiently.

The Bridge to Behavioral Theory

Over a period of time, it became apparent the era of scientific management concentrated heavily on productivity and little on the human aspect of management. The bridge to behavioral theory began to form with several theorists such as Mary Parker-Follett and Elton Mayo. Their studies and research led others to study the behavioral side of management.[20]

Scientific management proved to be an effective method for managing bureaucracies and complex organizations. However, it became obvious that management principles should also include the human aspect of keeping workers satisfied and productive. Theorists, Mary Parker-Follett and Elton Mayo bridged the gap between scientific management and the first group of behavioral theorists.

Mary Parker-Follett (1868-1933) believed that no one could become a whole person unless they became a member of a group. In this vein, the artificial distinction between managers and subordinates obscured the natural cohesion due to the designation of order givers and order takers. She believed traditional views should be abandoned and managers and subordinates should form in one group to accomplish the mission.

According to Parker-Follett, leadership should not come from formal authority, but from knowledge and experience. The manager would be the natural person to lead the group based on knowledge, not authority.[21]

Ms. Parker-Follett established herself as a political philosopher and scholar with her book entitled *"The Speaker of the House of Representatives"*. She was technically a member of the scientific management era, but became a member of the social era by generalizing the works of Taylor and anticipating many of the conclusions of the Hawthorne studies.[22]

Her 1924 book, *"Creative Experience"* suggested that through discussion and cooperation, people could manifest their unity in the pursuit of common goals. Integrative unity was the goal of group effort according to Follett.[23] Mary's response to group conflict was to hypothesize that a conflict of interest could be resolved in any of four ways:

1. Voluntary submission from one side
2. Struggle and the victory of one side
3. Compromise
4. Integration

Voluntary submission or struggle and victory from one side was unacceptable to Parker-Follett. She believed this practice represented the use of force or power. Compromise was futile because it served only to postpone the conflict until another time period. Therefore, according to Parker-Follett, integration involved finding a solution that was mutually agreed upon by both parties, and thus, gave it the best chance for success.[23]

Mary Parker-Follett is recognized for her research on the *"Law of the Situation"*. Simply stated, a manager has power over his/her employees if he/she has power with those employees. Business and unions were not willing to accept Parker-Follett's ideals because of their commitment to *"modus operandi"* and the comfort level they experienced in conflict as the key to change. Much time passed before collaborative and team building philosophies were accepted in the United States.

As management transitioned from the scientific management era, theorists such as Frank Gilbreth, Lillian Gilbreth, and Mary Parker-Follett convinced academia and industry that the human side of management was an important element in determining the functions of an organization. Three major theorists became the cornerstones of the behavioral era. Abraham Maslow, Frederick Herzberg, and Clayton

Alderfer developed separate, but similar models, to analyze human needs in the workplace. Their studies are discussed later in this introduction.

Elton Mayo (1880-1949) was born in Adelaide, South Australia and worked there until he was given a temporary position funded by Nelson Rockefeller at the University of Pennsylvania in 1923. He was educated at Harvard.[24]

Mayo's most significant research was conducted at Western Electric's Hawthorne Works from 1928 to 1932. MIT started the Hawthorne Study with Mayo spending 2 days in 1928, 4 days in 1929 and continuous research beginning in 1930.[7] In this study, Mayo was able to provide support for Mary Parker Follett's theory that far too little emphasis, by theorists, was placed on the human side of management.[25] Four different studies were conducted by Mayo, ranging in duration of months to several years.

The initial studies began as a study of the effects of light on productivity from 1924 to 1927. The primary reason for the studies was a desire by General Electric to sell more lights.[11] The light study showed no specific conclusions, but led researchers to believe that certain changes in work conditions would affect productivity. This belief prompted the need for the follow-up studies now famous as the *"Hawthorne Studies"*.[26]

Additionally, Mayo's research examined the effects of rest breaks on productivity.[27] He was interested in controlling the effects of monotony and fatigue through temperature, work hours, breaks, and other variables. To accomplish this, Mayo segregated six women and manipulated variables in the workplace. Throughout his experiment, Mayo changed work times, break times, lunch times, the length of activities, etc.

Mayo's experiments were conducted in series, changing part of the team when sessions changed. Throughout the experiment, supervisors kept the women informed of progress, asked them for advice, and listened to complaints. Detailed productivity records were kept through all phases.

The examined relay department normally produced approximately 2,400 relays each week. The workers were given a series of incentives. Each incentive produced increased productivity. When conditions were reversed to the original state, productivity rose to its highest level, surprising researchers.

The study indicated that recognizing employees and including them as contributing members of the organization will encourage workers to increase productivity. This result is very similar to the principles adapted by Deming as part of Total Quality Management (TQM). Mayo's theories of motivation are largely considered the beginning of human relations as a field of study.[28]

In 1984, Adair stated, "No other theory or set of experiments has simulated more research and controversy nor contributed more to a change in management thinking than the Hawthorne studies and the human relations movement it spawned".[29] The *"Hawthorne Effect"* is not always present as noted by a follow-up study known as the *"Bank Wiring Observation Room"* study that involved nine male workers. This group of employees had a preconceived notion of daily productivity and despite promises of greater incentives, refused to increase productivity.[30] This group dynamic could be likened to Irving Janis's study of group-think as peer pressure dictated productivity despite the best efforts of management.

Ironically, as experienced by both Taylor and Gantt, Mayo also experienced reluctant cooperation from disgruntled foremen encouraging workers to refer to past habits whenever Mayo was absent from experimental sites.[31]

Behavioral Era(1924-1952)

The **Behavioral Era** evolved due to the need for productivity coupled with organizational harmony.[20] As theorists studied increased productivity, the need for the human side of management became the focal point of this era. The *"Behavioral Era"* created the human relations movement, which produced numerous theories on how to balance employee relations with the goals of the organization.

Abraham Maslow's (1908-1970), *"Hierarchy of Needs"* became
a cornerstone of management thought and provided insight into behavior in the workplace. Maslow believed that employee needs fell into a hierarchy and each need should be satisfied in sequential order.[32] Maslow hypothesized that five needs exists within every individual.[32]

These include:

1. **Physiological**: Includes hunger, thirst, shelter, and other bodily needs

2. **Safety:** Includes security and protection for physical or emotional harm

3. **Social:** Includes affection, belongingness, acceptance, and friendship

4. **Esteem:** Includes internal esteem factors such as self-esteem, autonomy, and achievement and external esteem factors such as status, recognition, and attention

5. **Self-actualization:** The drive to become the best that one can be.

According to Maslow, no need is ever fully gratified; a substantially satisfied need no longer motivates. He believed that as each need is satisfied, the next need becomes dominant. Maslow separated the five needs into higher and lower orders.[32]

- Physiological, safety, social, and esteem needs were described as lower order needs
- Self-actualization as a higher order need

The first four areas in Maslow's hierarchy of employee needs are considered lower level needs. These are emotional needs that cause employees to exist on a daily basis. The social aspect effects an organization the most and is the one the organization has the most control over. It is important that employees are accepted by peers in the workplace. Conflict among employees becomes a business problem very quickly.

The last area in Maslow's hierarchy is an upper level need that addresses how employees feel about the company and their future with the company. Often, it is not employees that leave the companies causing problems. Disgruntled employees' that remain and sabotage a business by faulty or substandard work are the employees that harm an organization. So the question remains, what does a business owner do about motivation?

Companies should use knowledge derived from Maslow's *"Hierarchy of Needs"* to motivate employees. Employees are motivated in many ways, but obstacles can cause motivation to be impossible. Some of these conditions are controllable by management initiatives, while some motivating factors are well beyond internal control. Therefore, the more management knows about employees, the better they can manage.

The relationship is shown in *figure 3*.

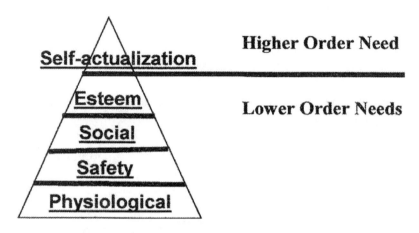

Figure 3 – *Maslow's "Hierarchy of Needs"*

When addressing the *"Hierarchy of Needs"* consider an employee in debt and his/her paycheck will not satisfy creditors. This employee is preoccupied with personal issues other than business. There may be personal problems occurring in an employee's life that is not work related, but affects productivity. An employee with a sick child, problem marriage, or disagreements with peers, will not be as productive as he/she would be with lesser worries.[32]

Managers should understand that employees' feelings play a large part in the success of your business. Convince employees the company cares by building motivation into the workplace. Provide positive leadership to the organization. Communicate in a positive manner how the business is doing and what the future might bring to the employees. Reassure employees about quality, future initiatives, and recently acquired contracts. Share and reinforce the organizational mission and vision with employees.

While there are far too many motivational techniques to list, a few examples include:

1) Have a system for compensation, raises, appraisals, rewards, hiring, and other human resource areas that is fair and equitable

2) Provide social outlets for your employees such as break-rooms, daycare (if possible), picnics, sports outings, etc.

3) Ensure the company does not discriminate against any group or gender in the organization

4) Provide professional development for your employees through training and a structure that allows for promotions and growth

5) Be fair and consistent in all aspects of management

Overall, there are numerous ways to motivate employees. Reassuring employees that management cares and making the workplace safe and secure are fundamental employee motivational measures. One positive systematic approach to management that ensures fairness will impress employees and promote positive attitudes.[32]

Clayton Alderfer reworked Maslow's *"needs"* hierarchy to align it with the empirical research. His revised need hierarchy is labeled *"ERG Theory"*. Alderfer argues there are three groups of core needs – existence, relatedness, and growth.[33]

1. The existence group: Providing our basic material existence requirements, which includes Maslow's physiological and safety needs.

2. Relatedness: The desire we have for maintaining important interpersonal relationships. These social and status desires require interaction with others. They align with Maslow's social need and the external component.

3. Growth needs: An intrinsic desire for personal development. These include the intrinsic component from Maslow's esteem category and the characteristics included in self-actualization.

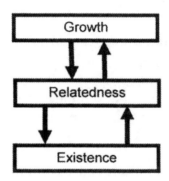

Figure 4 – *ERG Model*

Alderfer's "ERG"[33] theory also differs from Maslow's "Hierarchy of Needs",[32] in that:

1. More than one need may be operative at one time

2. If the gratification of a higher-level need is stifled, the need to satisfy a lower-level need increases

3. ERG theory does not assume that there exists a rigid hierarchy
4. A person can be working on growth even though existence and relatedness needs are not satisfied; or all three needs categories can be operative at the same time

5. ERG theory also contains a frustration-regression dimension. Maslow argued that an individual would stay at a certain need level until the need was satisfied. ERG theory notes that when a higher-order need level is frustrated; the individual's desire to increase the lower-level need is increased. ERG theory is more

consistent with our knowledge of individual differences among people.[33]

The *Two-factor theory* is sometimes called motivation-hygiene theory. Proposed by psychologist **Frederick Herzberg (1923-2000)** when he researched the question, "What do people want from their jobs?" Herzberg[34] addressed:

1. Intrinsic factors, such as advancement, recognition, responsibility, and achievement seem to be related to job satisfaction

2. Dissatisfied respondents tended to cite extrinsic factors, such as supervision, pay, company politics, and working conditions

3. The opposite of satisfaction is not dissatisfaction

4. Removing dissatisfying characteristics from a job does not necessarily make the job satisfying

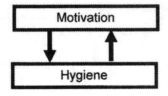

Figure 5 – *Herzberg's two factor model*

As depicted in *figure 5*, Herzberg's two factor theory broke behavior into two categories; motivation and hygiene.[35] The following are some elements of each:

Motivation factors:

- Achievement

- Recognition
- Responsibility
- Advancement
- Growth

Hygiene factors:

- Working conditions
- Salary
- Status
- Security
- Relations

Herzberg believed that job satisfaction factors are separate and distinct from job dissatisfaction factors. To motivate people, emphasize factors that are intrinsically rewarding and are associated with the work itself or to outcomes directly derived from it.[34]

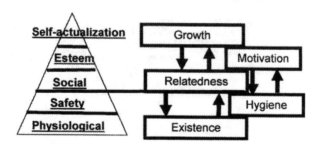

Figure 6 – *Synergy between Maslow, Alderfer, and Herzberg*

Although there are many philosophical differences, *Figure 6* shows the synergy between the three major behavioral models.

Transition Era

The *Transition Era* grew from a need to balance productivity with the human side of management. The pendulum of change swung from an emphasis on employee productivity to human relations over a period of years. This transition era attempted to balance the workplace with an effort to maintain productivity, while respecting the workforce.

W. Edwards Deming (1900 to 1993) introduced *"Total Quality Management (TQM)"* to Japan in the 1950's after it was rejected by the United States. This unique set of continuous process improvements changed Japan's inferior reputation for manufacturing quality to a reputation of setting world management standards.

In Japan, Deming introduced Statistical Process Control (SPC) and helped Japan earn a reputation for innovative, high quality products. Deming concentrated on managers and indicated that most quality problems resulted from poor management.[36]

While focusing on the customer, Deming concentrated on continuous process improvement, focusing on the customer through defect elimination, and management responsibility. In his book, Deming outlined 14 points for good management.[36] These included:

1. Create consistency of purpose toward improvement of product and service. Innovate, establish resources, and constantly improve.
2. Adopt a new philosophy. Refuse to accept defects.
3. Cease dependence on mass inspection. Inspection itself does not guarantee quality. Make individuals and managers responsible for quality.
4. End the practice of awarding business on the basis of price tag. Do not award contracts to the lowest bidder merely because they are the lowest bidder. Consistently improve supply chain management.

5. Improve constantly and forever the system of production and service. Treat each product as unique and build in quality at each point.
6. Institute training. Training should be a way of life in every organization. Additionally, training should vary as to reach people who learn differently.
7. Adopt and institute leadership. Hold managers accountable to lead, not merely supervise. Accountability and responsibility is an important element.
8. Drive out fear. Ensure workers are secure in their jobs and posses the ability to question management. Do not have too many rules.
9. Break down barriers between staff areas. Ensure the ability to boundary span is present in your company.
10. Eliminate slogans, exhortations, and targets for the work force. Instead, promote pride in personal workmanship to the point that an employee's work is their signature. Strive to eliminate defects.
11. Eliminate numerical quotas for the work force and management. Concentrate on a system that produces consistent improvement.
12. Remove barriers that rob people of pride of workmanship. Create a stabilized workforce where pride in workmanship can flourish.
13. Encourage education and self-improvement for everyone. Institute professional development and education into everyday life at your company.
14. Take action to accomplish this transformation. Managers are responsible for productivity. Manage through processes and ensure that measurement is a critical part of every task.

Source: *Chapter 2 of Deming, W.E. (1986). Out of Crisis. MIT Center for Advanced Engineering Study. Boston MA.*

Deming's 14 points are designed to improve every aspect of the workplace. Company growth will come from competitiveness through quality. Deming promoted quality in every aspect of productivity by ensuring workers were cared for and managers were responsible for results.[37]

Douglas McGregor (1906-1964) concluded that a manager's view of the nature of human beings is based on a certain grouping of assumptions. He developed a leadership theory termed *"Theory X and Theory Y"*.[38]

Theory X's assumptions were basically negative. They included:

1)   Employees inherently dislike work and, whenever possible, will attempt to avoid it
2)   Since employees dislike work, they must be coerced, controlled, or threatened with punishment
3)   Employees will avoid responsibilities and seek formal direction whenever possible
4)   Most workers place security above all other functions and will display little ambition

Theory Y's assumptions leaned toward the positive. They included:

1)   Employees can view work as being as natural as rest or play
2)   People will exercise self-direction and self-control if they are committed to the objectives
3)   The average person can learn to accept, even seek, responsibility
4)   The ability to make innovative decisions is widely dispersed throughout the population[39]

As depicted in *figure 7*, McGregor believed that Theory Y assumptions were more valid than Theory X assumptions.[38] Theory X assumes that lower-order needs dominate individuals. Theory Y assumes that people are dominated by higher-order needs.

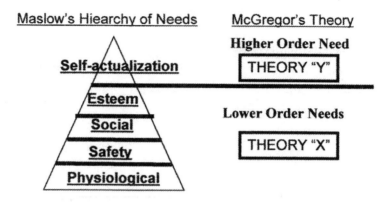

Figure 7 – *Synergy between Maslow's Hiearchy of Needs and McGregor's Theory X and Y*

In *"The Human Side of Enterprise"*,[38] McGregor described his views on leadership and his philosophy on Theory X and Theory Y. McGregor aligned himself with theorists, Mary Parker-Follett and Chris Argyis, by integrating the individual and organizational goals. While McGregor determined a perfect leader was not possible, he felt if a manager aligned himself with Theory Y, the organization would benefit. Therefore, improved industrial practice would result in increased efficiency and productivity.

Peter Drucker (1909-2005) provided the business community with Management by Objective (MBO). MBO is one of the most influential concepts developed and perfected by Drucker.[40]

MBO includes:

1) Directly advocates specific goals and feedback
2) Implies that goals must be perceived as feasible
3) Is most effective when the goals are difficult enough to require stretching
4) The only area of possible disagreement – participation

On November 11th 2005, management icon Peter Drucker died at the age of 95. Drucker's MBO impacted or changed the way business is conducted throughout the world. While some business owners may have never heard of Peter Drucker, successful owners and managers use his concepts.

Peter Drucker is known as the *"Father of Modern Management"* and his influence is evident over a seventy year time span. At the age of 94, Drucker wrote *"The Daily Drucker"* providing information on a vast array of topics including time management, outsourcing, and many issues.[41]

MBO is a structured management tool that sets goals for the organization. Each goal is jointly identified by management and employees. Expected results are determined from the beginning and agreed upon by all parties involved. Once the goal attainment process begins, management and employees meet regularly to measure success. Goals are adjusted, up or down, depending upon progress and results. This creates a mutually agreed upon direction for the company and keeps employees motivated.[40]

The MBO process begins with organizational goal setting. Drucker once noted that *"Management by objectives works – if you know the objectives." "Ninety percent of the time, you do not."* Therefore, the first step is to understand the organization's goals. Goals provide guidance to the organization, specifically to subordinate managers as they work with employees.[41]

Once organizational goals are determined and communicated, it is the manager's responsibility to work with employees, at every level, determining what goals will be used to meet strategic needs of the organization. Managers and employees should set goals in writing and record measurement for each goal.

Goals should be jointly reviewed on a routine basis. MBO is dependent upon employees understanding goals and committing to the success of the organization. Managers should provide as much autonomy as possible to allow goals to be accomplished, with freedom to work without interference. Employees must be held accountable for each goal.[40]

Critical key elements to Drucker's MBO are goal setting, measurement, timely execution, empowerment, and quality, all hallmarks of a successful business. Drucker's concept of MBO can be adapted and utilized by any organization. MBO works well with any corporate goal and is especially effective as an appraisal tool for your employees.

Peter Drucker's contributions to business did not end with MBO. Drucker wrote thirty-five books and hundreds of articles. During the 1940's Drucker studied the internal workings of General Motors Corporation and noted in his book *"Concept of the Corporation"* that employees needed empowerment and a level of independence if the company was to maintain continued growth.[41]

Drucker's identification of the *"knowledge worker"* was revolutionary for the time and predicted what we base our economy on today. A *"knowledge worker"* is someone using knowledge to analyze, maintain, manage, or manipulate data as a form of business. Drucker was a master at predictions regarding the future of management and had an uncanny talent for understanding the future. His wisdom helped each of us adapt to pending changes in the business environment.[12]

A business owner or manager can benefit by reading Drucker's management books. Drucker defined many concepts helpful to modern business. His desire to simplify operations and belief of never over producing, or hiring too many employees explains why many small businesses fail. Companies, moving too far from their core competencies tend to spread their management skills thin and cause unanticipated problems.

Drucker also described what he called *"planned abandonment"* as a method of sustaining business. His contention that businesses stayed with a product or service beyond its shelf life reflects how businesses have a tendency to ignore market changes.[12]

Overall, following the theories and concepts set forth by Peter Drucker will make your business competitive and sustainable. Management lost an icon on November 11th, 2005, but Peter Drucker's writings remain.

Herbert Simon (1916-2001) studied management by looking at

managers' sensitivities to certain types of problems and opportunities. Managers' can be aware of opportunities and still ignore them. Therefore, he determined there were limitations to rational problem solving. His bounded rationality model detailed how managers behave in organizational life. They make the most rational and logical decisions possible, limited by inadequate information and their ability to utilize the information.[42]

Herbert Simon became known as the *"Father of Quantitative Management"* by devising methodology for measurement of management decision-making. His thoughts on management theory included:

1)   There will be more conflict between units within a company sharing a common service unit than between those who do not.
2)   Innovation is most likely where incentives are tied directly to innovation; next most likely with companywide incentives and least likely with incentives for individual productivity.
3)   The more subordinates participate in policy decisions, the greater their sense of identification with the organization will be.

Rensis Likert (1903-1981)

Rensis Likert (1903-1981), like McGregor, Maslow, and Argyris, criticized modern human relations models as another way to manipulate employees. Likert felt that many factors motivated employees, not limited to money, such as positive performance and praise for good performance. In an effort to quantify attitude and opinion research, Likert developed the "Likert Scale", used today for survey measurement.[43]

Likert believed there should be a maximum probability in all interactions and in all relationships within an organization. Each member would view the experience as supportive and an experience to build and maintain his sense of personnel worth and importance. He analyzed mostly industrial organizations and different management styles. His contention that to optimize productivity, high profitability, and good relations with the workforce, a manager must maximize his/her human assets.[43]

According to Likert, management styles included:[44]

1. **Exploitive – authoritative system:** This system is directive, providing motivation through threats and intimidation. There is

40

very little communication and authority is at the senior management level.

2. **Benevolent – authoritative system:** leadership in this system is condescending and motivation is provided by rewards. This system provides very little communication and little teamwork. Authority is at the management level with employees having very little responsibility.

3. **Consultative System**: In this system authority is with management and very little trust is shared between managers and employees. Work is accomplished through some teamwork and communication. Motivation is accomplished by rewards and authority is shared, but mostly at the management level.

4. **Participative – group system:** In this system, managers have confidence in employees and share responsibility while maintaining authority. This system provides teamwork, communication, and participation. Administering rewards based on goals, drives, and motivation under this system.[44]

Likert believed the participative-group system was best for organizations that want to be successful. In order to convert an organization, Likert advocated that his four features of effective management be implemented.[45] These include:

1. Utilize modern principles and practices to motivate the workforce. Forget rewards and threats as a source of motivation.

2. Treat your employees as people who have wants, needs, standards, and values. Enhance the self-worth of your employees.

3. Create effective work groups and build a cohesive team that has a vested interest in the success of the company. Accomplish this through communication, goals and objectives.

4. Build mutual respect and supportive relationships among the workforce[45]

According to Likert, work groups should have solid leadership, tenure as a group, loyalty from both managers and employees, norms, values, goals, commitment to the company, and perform a task that is critical to the success of the company. If employees feel they are part of the solution, they will work harder to achieve the goals set forth by the company.[46]

Victor Vroom's (1932-   ) influence is felt by those who motivate
employees in the workplace. He was born in Canada in 1932 and earned a PhD. from the University of Michigan in 1958. Vroom is currently a faculty member at the Yale School of Management.

Vroom was instrumental in the field of motivation research by his work on the *"Expectancy Model"*. Simply stated, the expectancy model demonstrates that employees are motivated to work based on the probability of receiving a reward for the actions taken. Additionally, the employee's production is based on the belief that the productivity will be awarded by the organization.[47]

The expectancy model was developed in 1964 and designed specifically for use in the workplace. The model is based on the formula stating valence multiplied times expectancy (instrumentality) equals motivation.

Expectancy is based on the belief, by workers, that a productive act will be followed by a positive outcome. Valance is the value of the reward for the outcome. In Vroom's model, motivation is based on the workers attitude toward receiving a positive reward. If a worker does not care about reward, the theory will not work. The third element of Vroom's model is based upon is instrumentality. This is the belief that a manager will follow through with a reward if the positive act is accomplished.[47]

The belief that this model interacts psychologically to create a positive or negative motivational force drives the expectancy theory. Research by Vroom indicated that people work based on the need for pleasure or the avoidance of pain.[47] In 1968, Porter and Lawler modified the model to include relationships between motivation and abilities, traits, and role perception. They also distinguished between the reward being intrinsic or extrinsic.[48]

Victor Vroom continues to research motivation and has authored numerous papers and books.

Peter Senge (1947-   ) is the founder of the *Society for Organizational Learning (SOL)*. Senge is widely known for his work in the area of systems thinking, specifically organizational learning.[49]

In his 1990 book *"The Fifth Discipline: The Art and Practice of the Learning Organization"*, Senge describes learning organizations as "organizations where people continually expand their capacity to create the results they truly desire, where new and expansive patterns of thinking are nurtured, where collective aspiration is set free, and where people are continually learning how to learn together".[49]

In 1999, Senge was named *"Strategist of the Century"* by the Journal of Business Strategy for his work on defining, analyzing, and implementing the learning organization.[50] This prestigious award is given those who have the greatest impact on how we do business in the world today.

Senge's five learning disciplines of a learning organization include: *personal mastery, mental models, building a shared vision, team learning, and systems thinking.* The five disciplines speak directly to organizations coping with dynamic change in the business environment. The ability of organizations to learn and persuade their workers to continue learning is necessary for continued success. Senge's research on the learning organization helps managers understand, design, analyze, and function in a learning organization.[49]

The first learning discipline is *personal mastery.* This includes the discipline of clarifying the personal vision, focusing our energies, developing patience, and seeing reality objectively. Organizations are only as good as the people who work in them.

The second discipline is *mental models*. This includes assumptions, generalizations, or images that influence how we understand the world and how we take action. The ability of each employee to create a realistic model of the organizations role in the world will strengthen their ability to learn.

Building a shared vision is the ability of personnel in the organization to create a vision of the future the company seeks to create. This requires employees and leaders to commit to seeking a future that is agreed upon by all. The ability to understand where the company is going is critical to a learning organization.

The fourth discipline is *team learning*. The ability to learn as a team is crucial to productivity. Senge stresses that no matter how well individuals learn, it is the collective knowledge and abilities that drive a successful organization. He indicates that communication or "dialogue' is an important element in a learning organization. Senge believes that teams can accomplish far more than individuals.[49]

Systems thinking is the fifth discipline and involves the ability of management to view the organization in a holistic manner. A *"Systems Approach to Management"* refers to viewing the system as a *"whole"* to fully understand the parts of the system. According to Schoderbek, Schoderbek, & Kefalas, the *systems approach* implies that managers must depart from the traditional analytical approach to solve the more complex problems facing today's managers.[51] Managers must use systems thinking to develop a methodology for conceptualizing and implementing the systems approach. Several frameworks combine to make this possible.

Senge[49] defined several laws for implementing the practices necessary to create a learning organization. The first law of systems thinking is that *today's problems come from yesterday's solutions.*

Making decisions without completely analyzing the issue could cause an unanticipated problem.

Senge's second law is *the harder you push, the harder the system pushes back.* When managers are pushing too hard, they usually make the wrong decisions.[49] The complex business environment today will not tolerate hasty decisions without some form of complication. Hiring more employees to boost sales is usually counter productive. A systems approach would utilize improved processes to address the situation.

Behavior grows better before it grows worse is the third law of systems thinking. This law indicates that quick decisions without adequate analysis will show immediate results, but will not last for the long term.

The fourth law, *the easy way out usually leads back in,* explains the statement "we've always done it that way". This is common in organizations that do not adapt well to change.[49]

The fifth law of systems thinking is *the cure can be worse than the disease.* Organizations that apply short term solutions usually end up with more problems. Additionally, once the cure is in place it is very difficult to change. Therefore, an inadequate short term solution ends up as a poor long term correction.

Faster is slower constitutes the sixth law and refers to organization taking on more business than they can manage in the short term in order to gain business.[49]

According to Senge, the seventh law of systems thinking, *cause and effect are not closely related in time and space,* is based on the fact that problems are not necessarily caused by issues near by. In today's complex environment, a problem in a department located away from the company can cause issues in the system. In the systems holistic view, each sub-system affects the company as a whole.[49]

Senge's eighth law, *small changes can produce big results-but the areas of highest leverage are often the least obvious,* refers to viewing the system as a whole and thinking long term in your decision making process.[49]

The ninth law of systems thinking states that an organization *can have your cake and eat it too - but not at once.* Through this concept, an organization can obtain quality at a low cost, but not in the short term. A learning organization improves as it delivers its products or services over time.

The tenth law refers to organizations that downsize, when it is training and processes that need addressed.

The eleventh law, *dividing an elephant in half does not produce two small elephants,* speaks to the leadership and integrity of the company.[49]

There is no blame is Senge's twelfth and final law. There is no reason to blame outside factors when the problem is usually in the organization. Senge states that systems thinking shows us that there is no outside; you and the cause of your problems are part of a single system. The management of the firm is the first area to review when there is a problem.[49] Organizations operating in an environment of rapid change will be better served by adopting a systems approach to management.

A new concept that is attracting the attention of managers and academia is leading through emotional intelligence. Introduced by **Daniel Goleman (1946-   )**, founder of *Emotional Intelligent Services* and former writer for the New York Times, this theory is gaining credibility as a solution to leadership issues.[52]

Emotional intelligence considers a person's ability to understand themselves and management's ability to understand the emotional state of employees. This knowledge leads to positive relationships, understanding of issues, better diversity, and improved team building.

According to Goleman, emotional intelligence is defined as *"The capacity for recognizing our own feelings and those of others, for monitoring ourselves, and for managing emotions well in ourselves and in our relationships"*. Goldman adapted this theory from a proposal in 1990 by two psychologists, Peter Salovey and John Mayer.[52] Salovey and Meyer[53] described emotional intelligence as a method to utilize one's feelings and emotions to, "monitor and regulate emotions", and to use these skills to effectively manage the organization.[52]

Emotional intelligence is a complex modeling system that analyzes how individuals deal with stress and use this experience to improve productivity.[54] Emotional Intelligence models were perfected over several years, producing the four branches of emotional intelligence in 1997. The four branches of emotional intelligence include: perception, facilitation, understanding, and management. These models determined how individuals and managers control emotions in everyday management of their business.

The concept of emotional intelligence allows managers to understand natural emotions and use that knowledge to motivate, plan, and manage the organization. The ability for managers to process information allows managers to accurately identify emotions and use those emotions to help in the decision making process. People rated high in emotional intelligence should be capable of identifying emotional issues in the workplace quickly and work through them easily.[55]

The first element, *Perception,* is a measure for managers to identify emotion in the actions or expressions of employees. *Facilitation* is a management skill that utilizes emotions to aid in problem solving and reasoning. *Understanding* allows mangers to conceptualize how emotions affect relationships in the organization. The last element, *management,* provides the managers with skills to assimilate, perceive, and manage emotion in a way that improves the organization.[53] Together, the four elements help explain how managers can use emotional intelligence to improve relationships and management in the organization.

Emotions categorized by Goleman includes: anger, sadness, fear, enjoyment, love, surprise, disgust and shame.[56] All are present everyday in the workplace and produce either positive or negative energy.

Understanding emotional intelligence equips a manager to cope with family issues, depression, and diversity. Management by emotional intelligence is dependent upon managers' independence, interdependence, and hierarchical capacities. *Independence* describes the respect that managers' ability to make a solid contribution to the performance of subordinates. A strong ability to network constitutes *interdependence. Hierarchical* refers to how employees and managers depend upon each other and build on combined strengths.[52]

The emotional competence framework described by Goleman includes self-awareness, self-regulation, motivation, empathy, and social skills. The ability to manage one's self and others is based on this model.[52]

Self-awareness refers to the ability to recognize emotions and self assess. Also included is the level of *self-confidence* that provides individuals with the feeling of worth and confidence in their capabilities. A critical element is *self-regulation.* The ability to maintain self control and be conscientious is critical to productivity. Commitment, initiative, drive, and optimism are all indicators of *motivation.*

Empathy for others provides an incentive to develop those around you and serve the organization in a positive manner. The last element of this model is *social skills*. *Social skills* provide the ability to communicate, influence, lead, create change, build teams and manage conflict. The more you understand about yourself and your employees, the better you are equipped to manage productively.

Understanding the emotions of employees will enable managers to utilize them in a value added manner. Emotions are present at all times and anticipating reactions to decisions will increase acceptance.

Irving Janis (1918-1990) examined how an organization could be the victim of *group-think*. This is a process of group dynamics that can effect organizations at all levels. Irving Janis describes *group-think* as "a mode of thinking that people engage in when they are deeply involved in a cohesive group; when the members' strivings for unanimity override their motivation to realistically appraise alternative courses of action". The effects of group-think can be either positive or negative and can affect management as well as employees.[57]

Group-think exists in every level of the organization. Some theorists attribute well-known historical events such as the *Bay of Pigs* and the *Challenger* disaster to the affects of group-think. It is common for managers to exercise caution when telling the boss what he/she doesn't want to hear. In all organizations, areas of imperfection can be found and it can be difficult to know when to speak up or when to remain silent. You can do things wrong forever and only lose customers, but it only takes one mistake that can bankrupt your business. It's quite possible the financial situations Enron and WorldCom are examples of senior level group-think.[57]

At lower level management, group-think is usually the employees' attitudes and opinions concerning the company or the managers leading them. The goal in any company is to create positive group-think. Management's ability to develop a positive culture will enable employees to be innovative, creative, and therefore maintain a positive outlook. Unfortunately, group-think often surfaces as a negative phenomenon that affects the ability of the group to make decisions. Once the negative symptoms of group-think influence the company, it is difficult to reverse. Therefore, the company should strive to keep group-think positive, thus providing a significant impact in the organization.[57]

Whether positive or negative, group-think is probably an issue in your company. In order to understand group-think, it is important that you understand the symptoms. A few of the main systems are:

1. **Illusions of invulnerability** – a group feels that everything they do is right

2. **Collective rationalization** - anything that doesn't fit into the group's ideology is explained away or discredited

3. **Groups believe their decisions are morally correct** – the ethical consequences of decision-making are ignored

4. **Excessive Stereotyping** – groups build negative stereotypes for anyone outside of the group

5. **Pressure for conformity** – pressure is applied from within the group to anyone questioning the group's beliefs or commitments

6. **Self-censorship** – group members keep any dissenting thoughts to themselves

7. **Illusion of Unanimity** – group members feel that all members of the group agree with the thoughts and actions of the group

8. **Mind guards** – group members assume the role as enforcers by responding to any negative views that may change the group

As explained earlier, group-think can be positive or negative. Obviously, the symptoms above highlight the negative impact of group-think. As a manager, you can enlist group-think to work for you. Positive group-think allows employees to discuss your company enthusiastically with customers and coworkers. The positive culture created by this action is exactly what people strive to achieve.[57] Some methods of avoiding negative group-think include:

1. Communicate with the group and emphasize the consequences of group-think

2. Be willing to accept criticism and provide a forum for your employees to voice grievances, objections, and doubts

3. Allow employees to be innovative in decision-making situations. Provide opportunity for creativity for tasks and jobs delegated to junior leaders in the company

4. Assign the role of "devils advocate" to members of the company when in group situations

5. Divide work groups differently if feasible. Break from the norm and allow different employees to work together on teams

6. Pay attention to the warning symptoms of group-think

7. Allow workers to express doubts or concerns about decisions in the company

8. Bring in outside experts whenever feasible

9. Establish several groups to work on the same administrative issue. This allows for different views and open discussion.

Management Thought Conclusion

The theorists and management issues discussed are not inclusive and only represents a fraction of theorists and issues faced on a daily basis. However, establishing good practices that allow for open communication and self-esteem among the workforce will spread into other areas of the business, such as customer service and productivity. Positive employees, with a healthy attitude about the organization, will create a positive community image. In-tune, in-touch leadership is the key to productivity.

Henry Laurence Gantt and his friend Frederick Winslow Taylor

In his book *"The Dilbert Principle"*, Scott Adams stated "Employees are our number one asset" in his section on the "Great Lies of Management".[58] How many times have you heard managers, or worse yet, politicians use the cliché that their employees are "the best in the world". If this statement is not based on statistically analyzed measurement, it might not be true. Far too often, the statement is political and designed to bond a particular group to his/her cause.

Many times, managers are chastised as "hard to work with," tyrants. Often, they are merely trying to get employees to perform the job they were hired to do. Managers that require productivity are often told that employees are unhappy or feel threatened by their management style. While there are no perfect leaders, political support for managers is imperative in a successful company.

Gantt concentrates on the aspect of management supported by measurement. Currently, the *"Gantt Chart"* is used widely as a critical tool for project management. Throughout this introduction, the use of measurement emerges as a theme for winning the political battle and improving productivity.

Frederick Taylor gets most of the credit for early management thought and is defined by many as the *"Father of Scientific Management"*.[8] However, it was Henry Gantt who worked closely with Taylor and was instrumental in creating a system that provided a guaranteed wage and bonus process as an incentive for workers. As mentioned earlier, his "Gantt Chart" utilizes charts and graphs to schedule multiple tasks over time. Gantt's theories concentrate on positive work as motivation rather than punishment for poor productivity.

As we read Gantt's book, *"Organizing for Work"*,[13] it is important that we understand the lessons from Taylor's book, *"The Principles of Scientific Management."*[8] Both men were instrumental in forming the scientific management era, and therefore, molding our method of management in today's global environment.

Gantt used charts for everything possible and emphasized throughout his book that charts are an extremely important element to successful management. Gantt mentions:[13]

Page 17: "Following this general exposition of the subject, we shall show a system of progress charts which bear the same relation to the statistical reports which are so common that a moving picture film bears to a photograph. - If we chart everything we are doing that way, anybody can run the shop".

Management tools, such as the Gantt chart, supports management when employees use the political avenue to undermine the first line supervisor. Charts keep managers on target and provide valuable information for decision making.

The method utilized by early managers to overcome a political atmosphere is known as scientific management. Often, manager bashing is an attempt at obstructionism by employees with an agenda. Scientific management utilizes processes, measurement, and feedback, allowing senior management an opportunity to sort through character assassination and make decisions based on facts. The method utilized is scientific management, but the key is supportive senior leadership.

Frederick Taylor and Henry Gantt knew this very well. Management historians are well aware of these two late 1800's and early 1900's pioneers and their collective successes improving productivity. However, both agreed their theories could not be successful without total support of senior management. Taylor wrote of threats made on his life and family. Gantt refers to economic hardships due to employees not performing as required. This problem has existed for centuries. How managers deal with the situation is an important element to the future of our country as a world industry leader.

Frederick Taylor wrote:[8]

> Page 23: "The writer had two advantages, however, which are not possessed by ordinary foreman, and these came, curiously enough, from the fact that he was not the son of a working man".
> "First, owing to the fact that he happened not to be of working parents, the owners of the company believed that he had the interest of the works more at heart than the other workmen, and they therefore had more confidence in his word than they did in that of the machinists who were under him". Taylor used the example of the Superintendent believing machines were smashed by incompetent foreman overstraining them while the same Superintendent would accept the explanation from him that the machines were being deliberately broken to slow the piece-rate being produced".

> Page 24: "Second, if the writer had been one of the workmen, and lived where they lived, they would have

brought such social pressure to bear upon him that it
would have been impossible to have stood out against
them. He would have been called "scab" and other foul
names every time he appeared on the street, his wife
would have been abused, and his children would have
been stoned. Once or twice he was begged by some of
his friends among the workmen not to walk home, about
two and one-half miles along the lonely path by the side
of the railway. He was told that if he continued to do
this it would be at the risk of his life".

Taylor and Gantt were not anti-employee. Taylor believed that
employees should be compensated for their efforts. In fact, both Gantt
and Taylor advocated distribution of wealth between business owners
and employees. They believed that employees vested in the company
would work harder. Taylor notes:[8]

> Page 1: "The principal object of management should be
> to secure the maximum prosperity for the employer,
> coupled with the maximum prosperity for each
> employee".

Their ideas were slightly different from today's *"piece work"* or
"commission" system, but produced the same results. Taylor
advocated increased pay for increased productivity.

Taylor states:[8]

> Page 1: "The majority of these men believe that the
> fundamental interests of employees' and employers are
> necessarily antagonistic. Scientific management, on the
> contrary, has for its very foundation the firm conviction
> that the true interests of the two are one in the same; that
> prosperity for the employer cannot exist through a long
> term of years unless it is accompanied by prosperity for
> the employee, and visa versa; and that it is possible to

give the workman what he wants – high wages – and the employer wants – a low labor cost – for his manufacturers".

The scientific approach makes higher productivity possible by improving processes so that they are concise and measurable. Employees are held to an obtainable standard. This allows productive employees to prosper, while nonproductive employees are identified. These employees should be trained, counseled, or eliminated. Taylor and Gantt worked together to study productivity and increase efficiency. Their results were significant.

One famous experiment is the study of loading *"Pig Iron"*. In his book, Taylor outlines this success:[8]

Page 19: "Our first step was the scientific selection of the workman. In dealing with workmen under this type of management, it is an inflexible rule to talk to and deal with only one man at a time, since each workman has his own special abilities and limitations, and since we are not dealing with men in masses, but are trying to develop each individual man to his highest state of efficiency and prosperity. Out first step was to find the proper workman to begin with. We therefore carefully watched and studied these 75 men for three or four days, at which time we had picked our four men who appeared to be physically able to handle pig iron at a rate of 47 tons per day. A careful study was then made of each of these men. We looked up their history as far back as practicable and through inquiries were made as to the character, habits, and ambition of each of them. Finally we selected one from among the four as the most likely man to start with. He was a little Pennsylvania Dutchman who had been observed to trot back home for a mile or so after his work in the evening, about as fresh as he was when he came trotting down to work in the morning. We found that upon wages of $1.15 a day he had succeeded in buying a small plot of ground, and that he was engaged in putting up the walls of a little house for himself in the morning before he starting to work and at night after leaving. He also had the reputation of being exceedingly "close", that is, of placing a very high value on a dollar. As one man whom we talked to about him said, "A penny looks about the size of a cart-wheel to him". This man we will call Schmidt". "The task before us, then, narrowed itself down to getting Schmidt to handle 47 tons of pig iron per day (they handle 12 ½ tons per day now) and making him glad to do it".

"What I want to find out is whether you are a high-priced man or one of these cheap fellows here. What I want to find out is whether you want to earn $1.85 per day or whether you are satisfied with $1.15, just the same as those cheap fellows are making?"

Taylor successfully changed production by 270% per man. This equated to an increase from 12 ½ tons per day to 47 tons per day, while pay only increased by 38% from $1.15 to $1.85.

Taylor and Gantt wrote continuously about the importance of ensuring employees worked at their maximum capacity. However, they also noted that management should reward employees accordingly by distributing profits fairly and equally. Neither man displayed tolerance for substandard workers or greedy employers.

Employees' not performing up to established standards is as old as management. Taylor writes:[8]

Page 3: "Under working, that is, deliberately working slowly so to avoid dong a full day's work, *"soldiering"*, as it is called in this country, "hanging it out", as it is called in England, *"ca Canae"*, as it is called in

58

Scotland, is almost universal in industrial establishments, and prevails also to a large extent in the building trades; and the writer asserts without fear of contradiction that this constitutes the greatest evil with which the working people of both England and America are now afflicted".

Taylor understood there were many reasons for *"soldiering"*. Peer pressure, especially in unions, was an issue that must be dealt with by management regardless of the century. Taylor states:[8]

Page 5: "For every individual, however, who is overworked, there are a hundred who intentionally under work – greatly under work – every day of their lives, and who for this reason deliberately aid in establishing those conditions which in the end inevitably result in low wages".

Page 6: "This loafing or soldiering proceeds for two causes. First, from the natural instinct and tendency of men to take it easy, which may be called natural soldiering. Second, from more intricate second thought and reasoning caused by their relations with other men, which may be called systematic soldiering".

Page 7: "The writer was much interested recently in hearing one small but experienced gold caddy boy of twelve explaining to a green caddy, who had shown a special energy and interest, the necessity of going slow and lagging behind his man when he came up to the ball, showing him that since they were paid by the hour, the faster they went the less money they got, and finally telling him that if he went too fast the other boys would give him a licking".

Page 7: "This represents a type of systematic soldiering which is not, however, very serious, since it is done with the knowledge of the employer, who can quite easily break it up if he wishes. The greater part of systematic soldiering, however, is done by the men with the deliberate object of keeping their employers ignorant of how fast work can be done".

As you read *"Organizing for Work"*, please note that Gantt's focus is similar to Taylors, but with some differences. It must be noted that the book was written during World War I and many of his efficiencies relate directly to meeting the war effort. Additionally, Gantt did extensive research on the cost of conducting business and, more importantly, the high cost of inefficiency.

Considering, *"Organizing for Work"*, was written while the US was struggling to meet war demands lends some credence that Gantt was advocating a socialist system such as the one employed by the failed Soviet Republic. Gantt writes:[13]

Page 65: "In other words, industrial control is too often based on favoritism or privilege, rather than on ability. This hampers the healthy, normal development of industrialism, which can reach its highest development only when equal opportunity is secured to all, and when all reward is equitably proportioned to service rendered. In other words, when industry becomes democratic".

The truth is, Gantt was advocating customer service, fair wages for a day's labor, and management fairness. These management elements were used in an effort to provide maximum productivity in a time of war. While Gantt was associated with Taylor during his research, this book reflects some major differences in their focus. While Taylor concentrated heavily on individual worker productivity, Gantt focused on the interaction of individual productivity, organizational efficiency, and the economy together.

Addressing the question posed earlier, could Gantt, Taylor, Gilbreth, Fayol, Parker-Follett, and their fellow theorists, do well in today's business climate? The answer often lies in management and execution. The rest of this introduction discusses many of Gantt's thoughts and how they have been applied throughout the years.

Service is a concept that Gantt advocates continuously in his book. In the preface of his book Gantt writes:[13]

> Preface: "In order to resume our advance toward the development of an unconquerable democratic civilization, we must purge our economic system of all autocratic practices of whatever kind, and return to the democratic principle of rendering service, which is the basis for this wonderful growth".

There was no substitute for customer service according to Gantt's management theory. His contention that employees wishing to collect the maximum pay must deliver the best possible efficiency was coupled with an equally strong belief that businesses wishing to maintain profitability must deliver the best possible service. Gantt knew that customer service would win over greed. Currently, America's business schools are moving back to the same concept of social responsibility over profit. Gantt stated:[13]

> Page 14: "I say again, then, we have come to the Parting of the Ways, for a nation whose business system is based on service will in a short time show such advancement over one whose business system is operated primarily with the objective of securing the greatest possible profits for the investing class, that the latter nation will not be long in the running".

Page 15: "The lesson is this: the business system must accept its social responsibility and devote itself primarily to service, or the community will ultimately make the attempt to take over in order to operate it in its own interest".

One reason Gantt appeared to lean toward the socialist system, advocated by the Soviet Union, was his lack of confidence in greedy business owners. Gantt felt government could manage the organization better and would be less concerned with profit. Gantt's writings indicated Europe made this mistake and this was part of the reason that the world was at war. In chapter one, Gantt wrote:[13]

Page 6: "I say, before we have come to the Parting of the Ways, for we must not drift on indefinitely toward economic catastrophe such as Europe exhibits to us".

Page 7: "We all realize that any reward or profit that business arbitrarily takes, over and above that to which it is justly entitled for service rendered, is just as much the exercise of autocratic power and a menace to the industrial peace of the world, as the autocratic-military power of the Kaiser was a menace to international peace. This applies to Bolshevists as well as Bankers".

To illustrate his thoughts on government intervention, Gantt uses the example of finances at the Emergency Fleet Corporation. War made the circumstances different than usual, but Gantt advocated that disagreements about how profits should be distributed affects the community negatively and therefore, cannot be tolerated.

Page 8-9: Emergency Fleet Corporation - "Under stress of war, when it was clearly seen that a business and industrial system run primarily for profits could not produce the war gear needed, we promptly adopted a method of finance that was new to us. The federal government took over the financing of these corporations as were needed to furnish munitions for the war"

Gantt really did not advocate socialism or any of the "isms" of that era. However, he was concerned that activists believing in other forms of combining government and the economy would prevail if we could not improve on service. Gantt wrote:[13]

> Page 100: "Unless the industrial and business system can rapidly recover a sense of service and grant it in the first place, it is hard to see what the next few years may bring forth".

> Page 101: "One class believes that the answer comes in government ownership and government control of industries".

Gantt's motivation to improve service and efficiency is reflected throughout this book and based partially on his religious beliefs. Gantt wrote:[13]

> Page 108: "Reward according to service rendered is the only foundation on which our industrial and business system can permanently stand. It is a violation of this principle which has made the occasion for socialism, communism, and Bolshevism. All we need to defeat these "isms" is to re-establish our industrial and business system firmly on the principles advocated by Abraham Lincoln in 1847, and we shall establish an economic democracy that is stronger than any autocracy".

> Page 109: "Now, however, when a great catastrophe has shown us the error of our ways, and convinced us that the world is controlled by deeds rather than words, we see the road to Universal Peace only through the change

of Christianity from a weekly intellectual diversion to a daily practical reality".

Gantt made a distinction between those who managed for profit and those who managed for productivity. This distinction applies to current managers who often forget successful manager's practices in a booming economy. Often, customer service and measuring costs become afterthoughts as managers assume that high sales will always be there. Gantt wrote:[13]

> Page 20: "The reason for its falling short is undoubtedly that the men directing it had been trained in a business system operated for profits, and did not understand one operated solely for production. This is no criticism of the men as individuals; they simply did not know the job, and, what is worse, they did not know they did not know it".

The current economy in most sectors of the country is growing, with many businesses having more customers than ever before. Unfortunately, fast economic growth is often accompanied by poor customer service in many organizations. This poor quality customer service is an issue that must be addressed by managers, as it occurs, not after the fact. The businesses that plan for growth by improving customer service are the ones that will remain competitive when the economy subsides.

It is unfortunate, as consumers, we tolerate poor customer service and inferior quality from many of the businesses we frequent. Today's fast-paced world often dictates that we do business out of convenience rather than quality. Although not always intentional, businesses take advantage of this compromise by treating the customer with indifference; not recognizing the fact that customers can go elsewhere.

However, no matter how unique an idea or product is, there will soon be competition. Even though the economy is growing, businesses competing for the market are also growing in numbers. Consumers have more choices than ever. Businesses must change their business strategy if they intend to maintain their percent of the market.

This creates unique problems for management in many respects. Maintaining ten percent of a large market may be better than fifty percent of a small market. When the market grows, the demand for goods and services are too often stretched to the point that quality suffers. A strategy that attempts to control as much of the market as possible may result in providing an inferior product. Contracting for a major purchase and then discovering the sales pitch was drastically different than the delivered service or product is a prevalent problem in business. Promising a service or product that cannot be delivered is never a good idea. Yet, in a growing economy, it is human nature to want all of the business available.

Gantt wrote this about service versus profits:[13]

> Page 4-5: "The Sherman Anti-Trust law was the first attempt to curb this tendency". (Putting profits before service) "It was, however, successful only to a very limited extent, for the idea that profits of a business were justified only on account of the service it rendered was rapidly giving way to one in which profits took the first place and service the second".

Business owners who pay attention to operations by ensuring quality customer service will be successful businesses. Some of the best practices include:

1. Leadership – Customer service starts at the top and filters down, not the other way around. Positive leadership helps establish and enforce quality standards.

65

2. Deliver a quality product – Whether it is a good or service, pay close attention to the quality of the product. A satisfied customer will tell ten people, but an unhappy customer will tell fifty.

3. Know the customer base – Pay attention to everything about your customers. If the company loses a customer, find out why. Understand the strengths and weaknesses of the company through customers. Surveys, interviews, and daily conversations are great tools for gathering this information.

4. Generate a positive image – Word of mouth advertising is by far the best and least expensive advertising a company can have. Make it a policy to retain every customer that walks through the doors.

5. Get employees involved – Hold meetings where the agenda is customer service. Talk about the processes that work and those that are not so successful.

6. Make a quality customer service checklist – Work with employees to create the top ten points of service in the business. Make it part of the culture to emphasize customer service at all times.

7. Measure customer service – Keep records of complaints, recommendations, sales, good comments, returns, etc. Use the accumulated data to make adjustments.

8. Add staff when necessary – Maintain quality by keeping pace with new business. Waiting too long to hire additional personnel will cause a company to lose existing employees and customers.

This list is definitively not inclusive, but if Gantt's book is seriously considered, these management practices are still applicable in today's business environment. As in the days of the scientific management era, there are numerous practices that lead to improved customer service. If a company makes customer service a priority and employees understand the goals, success will occur in the business. Gantt shared Taylor's concern regarding inefficient workers. While Gantt did not spend too much time on this issue, he was concerned about idle workers and idle capital. It did not matter why, only that management was allowing productivity to slip. Gantt wrote:[13]

> Page 25: "Another phase of the efficiency movement with which we are all so familiar, was the attempt to increase the efficiency of the worker, and to completely ignore the idler, because the system of cost-keeping generally in vogue made that seem the most profitable thing to do. The case was worse that this, for not only did the system ignore the idler, but it eliminated the inefficient, absolutely ignoring the fact that both the inefficient and the idle were going to continue to live and be supported, directly or indirectly, by the workers".

> Page 26: "This leads us at once to two natural questions: What is our expense for idle labor? What is our expense for idle capital?

The answers to the two questions are critical, yet many managers fail to even ask the questions. The ability of managers to measure data, then use that information for effective decision making was important to Gantt and other management theorists as it is to modern managers. Gantt wrote:[13]

> Page 28: "While it is possible to get quite accurately the amount of material and labor used directly in the production of an article, and several systems have been

devised which accomplish this result, there does not yet seem to be in general use any system of distributing that portion of the expense known variously as indirect expense, burden, or overhead, in such a manner as to have any real confidence that it has been done properly".

Gantt had no knowledge of the many tools available to today's managers. If he were fortunate enough to manage today, he would probably be amazed. Beginning with the management tool that he made famous, the Gantt Chart, and including today's software products, there is no reason for management not to measure and make excellent use of data collected.

The process selected for charting is an individual decision. Standard flowcharting techniques utilize a start point, process point, decision point, report identifier, and a stop or connection element. This allows the team to identify every step in the process. The most important stage in the process is the situational exception reports, allowing managers' to spot-check the process at various points in the process. Once the flowcharting process is complete, evaluate the process for alternatives, inspection points, and methods to improve the process. This is a continuous methodology that will improve your operation and training.

Gantt was a pioneer in the area of charting. Gantt wrote this about the use of charts to improve activities:[13]

Page 81: "Figure 6 (an early Gantt Chart shown in the book) is a sample of the charts referred to above. This is an actual Ordinance Department chart, entered up to the end of December, 1917, the names of the items being replaced by letters. It was used to illustrate the methods employed and to instruct people in the work".

Page 83: "From the illustrations given the following principles upon which the chart system is founded are easily comprehended:

First: The fact that all activities can be measured by the amount of time needed to perform them.

Second: The space representing the time unit on the chart can be made to represent the amount of the activity which should have taken place in that time.

Bearing in mind these two principles, the whole system is readily intelligible and affords a means of charting all kinds of activities, the common measure being time".

Conclusion

One last consideration on charting to keep in mind! Peter Drucker once said, "There is surely nothing as useless as doing with great efficiency what should not be done at all".[12] Remember this quote and emphasize the critical elements of your business.

As you read the Gantt book, please be mindful that Gantt's systematic management is not that different from what we should be practicing today. His work ethic is often sought in today's managers. Although most work environments are far more complicated than in the early 1900's, following his example will be as successful today as it was in his day.

Endnotes

1. Ackman, D. (2002, March 22). *Pay madness at Enron*. Retrieved January 30, 2006, from http://www.forbes.com/2002/03/22/0322enronpay.html
2. Staff. (2005, April 27). *More GM layoffs, closings possible*. USA Job News. Retrieved January 22, 2006, from http://www.usajobs.org/viewarticle.jsp?articleuid=1115277 4131571027493607
3. Editorial (2006, January 31). The Waterbury Connecticut Republic American Newspaper. Retrieved January 30, 2006, from http://www.rep-am.com/story.php?id=2297
4. Chang, H.K. (2003, October). What led to Enron, WorldCom and the like? Retrieved January 30, 2006, fromhttp://www.gsb.stanford.edu/news/headlines/2003alu mniwkend_mcnichols.shtml
5. Suarez, Ray. (2002, September 2002). *Executive perks*. Retrieved January 24, 2006, from http://www.pbs.org/newshour/bb/business/july-dec02/perks_09-16.html
6. Gantt, H.L. (1919). *Organizing for work*. New Jersey: Hardcourt, Brace & Howe, Inc. The Quinn & Boben Company.
7. Wren, Daniel A., (1994). *The evolution of management thought*, 4th ed., John Wiley & Sons, Inc. , New York.
8. Taylor, F.W. (1911). The principles of Scientific Management. Dover Publications, Copyright 1998. Original published by New York: Harper & Bros., 1911.
9. Bass, B.M. (1981). *Stogill's handbook of leadership* (Rev. ed.). New York: The Free Press.
10. Wrege, C.D., & Perroni, A.G. (1974, March). Taylor's Pig-Tale: A Historical Analysis of Frederick W. Taylor's Pig-Iron Experiments. *Academy of Management Journal, 17*(1).

11. Wren, Daniel A., and Greenwood, Ronald G., (1996). *Management Innovators: The people and ideas that have shaped modern business.* Oxford University Press, Inc., New York.

12. Drucker, P.F. (1976). *The coming rediscovery of scientific management.* The Conference Board Record.

13. Gantt, H.L. (1916). *Industrial Leadership.* New Haven, Connecticut: Yale University Press.

14. GANTT http://en.wikipedia.org/wiki/Gantt_chart, retrieved from the Web Feb 20, 2006

15. Gilbreth, L. (1914). *The psychology of management.* New York: Sturgis & Walton Publishers.

16. Fayol, H. (1930). *General and industrial management.* Reprinted by El Ateno, Paris France. Copyright 1994. Original published by Pitman and Sons, ltd., 1916.

17. Weber, M. (1947). *The theory of social and economic organization.* New York: Oxford University Press.

18. Weber, M. (1946). *The sociology of charismatic authority.* In Mills, H.H., & C.W. Mills (Eds. and Trans.). *From Max Weber: essays in sociology.* New York: Oxford University Press.

19. Bendixs. R. (1960). *Max Weber: An Intellectual Portrait.* New York: Doubleday Book

20. Stodgill & Bass (1981)

21. Parker-Follett, M. (1918). *The New State: Group Organization the Solution of Popular Government.* London: Longmans, Green, & Company.

22. James, E.T. (1971). *Notable American Women: A Biographical Dictionary.* Cambridge, MA: Harvard University Press 639 – 641.

23. Parker-Follett, M. (1924). *Creative Experience.* London: Longmans, Green, & Company.

24. Smith, J.H. (1998, March). The enduring legacy of Elton Mayo. *Human Relations, 51*(3), 221 – 250.

25. Rieger, B.J. (1995). Lessons in productivity and people. *Training and Development Journal: 49*(10), 1 – 2.

26. Carey, A. (1967). The Hawthorne studies: A radical criticism. *American Sociological Review, 32,* 403-416.
27. Mayo, E. (1933). *The human problems of an industrial civilization.* New York: Viking Press.
28. Dingley, J.C., & Durkelm. (1997). Mayo, morality and management. *Journal of Business Ethics, 16*(11), 1 – 18.
29. Adair, J.G. (1984). The Hawthorne effect: A reconsideration of the mythological artifact. *Journal of Applied Psychology, 69*(2), 334 – 345.
30. Roethlisberger, F.J. & Dickson, W.J. (1939). *Management and the Worker: An account of a research program conducted by the Western Electric Company, Hawthorne Works, Chicago.* Cambridge MA: Harvard University Press.
31. Rose, M. (1975). *Industrial behavior.* Harmondsworth: Penguin Publishers.
32. Maslow, A.H. (1954). *Motivation and personality.* New York: Harper & Rowe.
33. Alderfer, C.P. (1972). *Existence, relatedness, and growth: human needs in organizational settings.* New York: The Free Press.
34. Herzberg, F. (1966). *Work and the Nature of Man.* New York: World Publishing.
35. King, N. (1970). Clarification and Evaluation of the Two-Factor Theory of Job Satisfaction. *Psychological Bulletin.* Vol. 74, no. 1, pp. 18-31.
36. Deming, W.E..(1986). *Out of Crisis.* MIT Center for Advanced Engineering Study.
37. Getlow, H.S. & Gitlow, S.J. (1989). *The Deming guide to quality and competitive position.* New Jersey: Prentice Hall Publishers.
38. McGregor, D. (1964). *Leadership and motivation.* Cambridge MA: M.I.T. Press.
39. McGregor, D. (1960). *The human side of management.* New York: McGraw-Hill Publishing.
40. Drucker, P.F. (1954). *The practice of management.* New York: Harper.

41. Drucker, P.F. (1946). Concept of the corporation. New York: John Day.
42. Simon, H.A. (1976). *Administrative Behavior.* New York: MacMillan Publishing Company.
43. Likert, R. (1967). *The human organization.* New York: McGraw-Hill Publishing.
44. Likert, R. (1977a). Management styles and the human component. *Management review, 66,* 23-45.
45. Likert R. (1977b). *Past and future perspectives on system 4.* Proceedings of the Academy of Management.
46. Likert, R. (1975). *Improving cost performance and cross-functional teams.* Conference Board. Record, 92, 51-59.
47. Vroom, V. (1964). *Work and motivation.* New York: Wiley Publishing.
48. Porter, L.W. & Lawler, E.F. (1968). *Managerial attitudes and performance.* Homewood, IL: Dorsey Press.
49. Senge, Peter. (1990). *The Fifth Discipline: The Art and Practice of the Learning Organization"*
50. Journal of Business Strategy (September/October 1999).
51. Schoderbek, P.P., Schoderbek, C.G., & Kefalas, A.G. (1990). *Management Systems, Conceptual Considerations.* Irwin Publishing Company.
52. Goleman, D. (1998). *Working with Emotional Intelligence.* New York: Bantam Books Publishers.
53. Salovey, P. & Mayer, J.D. (1990). Emotional Intelligence. *Journal of Imagination, Cognition, and Personality, 9,* 185 – 211.
54. Salovey, P., Hsee, C., & Mayer, J.D. (1993). Emotional intelligence and the self-regulation of affect. In D.M. Wegner & J.W. Pennebaker (Eds.) Handbook of mental control (pp. 258-277). Englewood Cliffs, NJ: Prentice Hall.
55. Mayer, J.D., & Salovey, P. (1997). *What is emotional intelligence?* In Salovey, P., & Sluyter, D. (Eds). Emotional Development and Emotional Intelligence: Implications for Educators, 3 -31. New York: Basic Books.

56. Goleman, D. (1994). *Emotional Intelligence: Why it can matter more than IQ.* New York: Bantam Books Publishers.
57. Janis, I.L. (1972). *Victims of group-think.* Boston: Houghton Mifflin.
58. Adams, Scott. (1996). *"The Dilbert Principle".*

Works Cited

Davenport, T.H. & Short, J.E. (1990, Summer). The new industrial engineering: information technology and business process redesign. *Sloan Management Review,* 11 -27.
Likert, R. (1973). Human resource accounting: building and assessing productive organizations. *Personnel, 50,* 8-24.

Organizing for Work

By

Henry Laurence Gantt

PREFACE

THE two greatest forces in any community are the economic force and the political force backed by military power. To develop the greatest amount of strength for the benefit of the community, they must work together, hence must be under one direction.

Germany had already accomplished this union before entering the war by having her political system practically take over the industrial, and the Allies rapidly followed suit after the war began.

"We also found soon after entering the war that our political system alone was not adequate to the task before it, and supplemented it by a food administrator, a coal administrator, a war labor board, a war industries board, a shipping board, and others, which were intended to be industrial, and as far as possible removed from political influences. There is no question that they handled their problems much more effectively than was possible under strictly political control. The Soviet system is an attempt to make the business and industrial system serve the community as a whole and in doing- so to take over the functions of and entirely supplant the political system. Whether it can be made to work or not remains to be seen. Up to date it has failed, possibly because the control has fallen into the hands of people of such extreme radical tendencies that they would probably wreck any system.

The attempt which extreme radicals all over, the world are making to get control of both the political and business systems on the theory that they would make the industrial and business system serve the community, is a real danger so long as our present system does not accomplish that end; and this danger is real irrespective of the fact that they have as yet nowhere proved their case.

Is it possible to make our present system accomplish this end? If so, there is no excuse for such a change as they advocate, for the great industrial and business system on which our modern civilization depends is essentially sound at bottom, having grown up because of the service it rendered. Not until it realized the enormous power it had acquired through making itself indispensable to the community did it go astray by making the community serve it. It then ceased to render service democratically, but demanded autocratically that its will be done. "It made tools and weapons of cities, states, and empires." Then came the great catastrophe.

In order to resume our advance toward the development of an unconquerable democratic civilization, we must purge our economic system of all autocratic practices of whatever kind, and return to the democratic principle of rendering service, which was the basis of its wonderful growth.

Unless within a short time we can accomplish this result, there is apparently nothing to prevent our following Europe into the economic confusion and welter which seem to threaten the very existence of its civilization.

Chapter 1 - THE PARTING OF THE WAYS

MODERN civilization is dependent for its existence absolutely upon the proper functioning of the industrial and business system. If the industrial and business system fails to function properly in any important particular, such, for instance, as transportation, or the mining' of coal, the large cities will in a short time run short of food, and industry throughout the country will be brought to a standstill for lack of power. It is thus clearly seen that the maintenance of our modern civilization is dependent absolutely upon the service it gets from the industrial and business system.

This system as developed throughout the world had its origin in the service it could and did render the community in which it originated. With the rise of a better technology it was found that larger industrial aggregations could render better and more effective service than the original smaller ones, hence the smaller ones gradually disappeared leaving the field to those that could give the better service.

Such was the normal and natural growth of business and industry which obtained its profits because of its superior service. Toward the latter part of the nineteenth century it was discovered that a relatively small number of factories, or industrial units, had replaced the numerous mechanics with their little shops, such as the village shoemaker and the village wheelwright, who made shoes and wagons for the community, and that the community at large was dependent upon the relatively smaller number of larger establishments in each industry.

Under these conditions it was but natural that a new class of business man should arise who realized that if all the plants in any industry were combined under one control, the community would have to accept such service as it was willing to offer, and pay the price which it demanded. In other words, it was clearly realized that if such combinations could be made to cover a large enough field, they would no longer need to serve the community but could force the community to do their bidding. The Sherman Anti-Trust Law was the first attempt to curb this tendency. It was, however, successful only to a very limited extent, for the idea that the profits of a business were justified only on account of the service it rendered was rapidly giving way to one in which profits took the first place and service the second. This idea has grown so rapidly and has become so firmly imbedded in the mind of the business man of today, that it is inconceivable to many leaders of big business that it is possible to operate a business system on the lines along which our present system grew up; namely, that its first aim should be to render service.

It is this conflict of ideals which is the source of the confusion into which the world now seems to be driving headlong. *The community needs service first, regardless of who gets the profits, because its life depends upon the service it gets.* The business man says profits are more important to him than the service he renders; that the wheels of business shall not turn, whether the community needs the service or not, unless he can have his measure of profit. *He has forgotten that his business system had its foundation in service, and as far as the community is concerned has no reason for existence except the service it can render.* A. clash between these two ideals will ultimately bring a deadlock between the business system and the community. The "laissez faire" process in which we all seem to have so much faith, does not promise any other result, for there is no doubt that industrial and social unrest is distinctly on the increase throughout the country.

I say, therefore, we have come to the *Parting of the Ways,* for - we must not drift on indefinitely toward an economic catastrophe such as Europe exhibits to us. We probably have abundant time to revise our methods and stave off such a catastrophe if those in control of industry will recognize the seriousness of the situation and promptly present a positive program which definitely recognizes the responsibility of the industrial and business system to render such service as the community needs. The extreme radicals have always had a clear vision of the desirability of accomplishing this end, but they have always fallen short in the production of a mechanism that would enable them to materialize their vision.

American workmen will prefer to follow a definite mechanism, which they comprehend, rather than to take the chance of accomplishing the same end by the methods advocated by extremists. In Russia and throughout Eastern Europe, the community through the Soviet form of government is attempting to take over the business system in its effort to secure the service it needs. Their methods seem to us crude, and to violate our ideas of justice; but in Russia they replaced a business system which was rotten beyond anything we can imagine. It would not require a very perfect system to be better than what they had, for the dealings of our manufacturers with the Russian business agents during the war indicated that graft was almost the controlling factor in all deals. The Soviet government is not necessarily Bolshevistic nor Socialistic, nor is it political in the ordinary sense, but industrial. It is the first attempt to found a government on industrialism. Whether it will be ultimately successful or not, remains to be seen. While the movement is going through its initial stages, however, it is unquestionably working great hardships, which are enormously aggravated by the fact that it has fallen under the control of the extreme radicals. Would it not be better for our business men to return to the ideals upon which their system was founded and upon which it grew to such strength; namely, that reward should be dependent solely upon the service rendered, rather than to risk any such attempt on the part of the workmen in this country, even if we could keep it clear of extreme radicals, which is not likely? *We all realize that any reward or profit that business arbitrarily takes, over and above that to which it is justly entitled for service rendered, is just as much the exer-* cise of autocratic power and a menace to the industrial peace of the world, as the autocratic military power of the Kaiser was a menace to international peace. This applies to Bolshevists as well as to Bankers.

I am not suggesting anything new, when. I say reward must be based on service rendered, but am simply proposing that we go back to the first principles, which still exist in many rural communities where the newer idea of big business has not yet penetrated. Unquestionably many leading business men recognize this general principle and successfully operate their business accordingly. Many others would like to go back to it, if they saw how such a move could be accomplished.

Under stress of war, when it was clearly seen that a business and industrial system run primarily for profits could not produce the war gear needed, we promptly adopted a method of finance which was new to us. The Federal Government took over the financing of such corporations as were needed to furnish the munitions of war. The financing power did not expect any profit from these organizations, but attempted to run them in such a manner as to deliver the greatest possible amount of goods.

The best known of these is the Emergency Fleet Corporation. It is not surprising that such a large corporation developed in such great haste should have been inefficient in its operating methods, but there are reasons to believe that it will, in the long run, prove to have handled its business better than similar undertakings that were handled directly through the Washington bureaus. It gave us a concrete example of how to build a Public Service corporation, the fundamental fact concerning which is that it must be *financed by public money.* That it has not been more successful is due, not to the methods of its financing, but to the method of its operation. The sole object of the Fleet Corporation was to produce ships, but there has never been among the higher officers of the Corporation a single person, who, during the past twenty years, has made a record in production. They have all without exception been men of the "business" type of mind who have made their success through financiering, buying, selling, etc. If the higher officers of the Fleet Corporation had been men who understood modern production methods, and had in the past been successful in getting results through their use, it is probable that the Corporation would have been highly successful, and would have given us a good example of how to build an effective Public Service corporation. Mr. William B. Colver, Chairman of the Federal Trade Commission, in the summer of 1917, explained how we might have a Public Service corporation for the distribution of coal. In such a corporation as Mr. Colver outlined, there •would be good pay for all who rendered good service, but no "profit." Of course, all those who are now making profits over and above the proper reward for service rendered in the distribution of coal, opposed Mr. Colver's plan, which was that a corporation, financed by the Federal Government, should buy at the mouth of each mine such coal as it needed, at a fair price based on the cost of operating that mine; that this corporation should distribute to the community the coal at an average price, including the cost of distribution. We see no reason why such a corporation should not have solved the coal problem, and furnished us with an example of how to solve other similar problems. We need such information badly, for we are rapidly coming to a point where we realize that *disagreements between employer and employee as to how the profits shall be shared can no longer be allowed to work hardship to the community.*

The chaotic condition into which Europe is rapidly drifting by the failure of the present industrial and financial system, emphasizes the fact that in a civilization like ours the problems of peace may be quite as serious as the problems of war, and the emergencies created by them therefore justify the same kind of action on the part of the government as was justified by war.

Before proper action can be taken in this matter it must be clearly recognized that today economic conditions have far more power for good or for evil than political theories. This is becoming so evident in Europe that it is impossible to fail much longer to recognize it here. The revolutions which have occurred in Europe and the agitation which seems about to create other revolutions, are far more economic than political, and hence can be offset only by economic methods.

The Labor Unions of Great Britain, and the Soviet System of Russia, both aim, by different methods, to render service to the community, but whether they will do it effectively or not is uncertain, for they are revolutionary, and a revolution is a dangerous experiment, the result of which cannot be foreseen. The desired result can be obtained *without a revolution* and by methods with which we are already familiar, if we will only establish real public service corporations to handle problems which are of most importance to the community, and realize Inasmuch as the profits in any corporation go to those who finance that corporation, the only guarantee that a corporation is a real public service corporation is that it is financed by public money. If it is so financed all the profits go to the community, and if service is more important than profits, it is always possible to get a maximum service by eliminating profits.

This is the basis of the Emergency Fleet •Corporation, and numerous other war corporations, which rendered such public service as it was impossible to get from any private corporations. Realizing that on the return of peace many private corporations feel that they have no longer such social responsibilities as they cheerfully accepted during the war, it would seem that real public service corporations would be of the greatest possible advantage in the industrial and business reorganization that is before us.

We have in this country a little time to think, because economic conditions here are not as acute as they are in Europe, and because of the greater prosperity of our country. But we must recognize the fact that our great complicated system of modern civilization, whose very life depends upon the proper functioning of the business and industrial system, cannot be supported very much longer unless the business and industrial system devotes its energies as a primary object to rendering the service necessary to support it. We have no hesitation in saying that the workmen cannot continue to get high wages unless they do a big day's work. *Is it not an equally self-evident fact that the business man cannot continue to get big rewards unless he renders a corresponding amount of service?* Apparently the similarity of these two propositions has not clearly dawned upon the man with the financial type of mind, for the reason, perhaps, that he has never compared them.

Such a change would produce hardships only for those who are getting the rewards they are not earning. It would greatly benefit those who are actually doing the work.

In order that we may get a clear conception of what such a condition would mean, let us imagine two nations as nearly identical as we can picture them, one of which had a business system which was based upon and supported by the service it rendered to the community. Let us imagine that the other nation, having the same degree of civilization, had a business system run primarily to give profits to those who controlled that system, which rendered service when such service increased its profits, but failed to render service when such service did not make for profits. To make the comparison more exact, let us further imagine a large portion of the most capable men of the latter community engaged continually in a pull and haul, one against the other, to secure the largest possible profits. Then let us ask ourselves in what relative state of economic development these two nations would find themselves at the end of ten years? It is not necessary to answer this question.

I say again, then, we have come to the *Parting of the Ways,* for a nation whose business system is based on service will in a short time show such advancement over one whose business system is operated primarily with the object of securing the greatest possible profits for the investing class, that the latter nation will not be long in the running.

America holds a unique place in the world and by its traditions is the logical nation to continue to develop its business system on the line of service. What is happening in Europe should hasten our decision to take this step, for the business system of this country is identical with the business system of Europe, which, if we are to believe the reports, is so endangered by the crude efforts of the Soviet to make business serve the community.

The lesson is this: the business system, must accept its social responsibility and devote itself primarily to service, or the community will ultimately make the attempt to take it over in order to operate it in its own interest.

The spectacle of the attempt to accomplish this result in eastern Europe is certainly not so attractive as to make us desire to try the same experiment here. Hence, we should act, and act quickly, on the former proposition.

Chapter 2 - THE ENGINEER AS THE INDUSTRIAL LEADER

THE principles explained in the preceding chapter may seem to be sufficiently clear and simple to appeal to almost any enlightened person, and give him the desire to carry them out. The desire to put them in operation, however, is not enough. He must have at least some inkling of the methods by which their application can be made. He must understand the forces with which he will have to contend in introducing the newer methods; the arguments that will be brought up against them, and the obstacles that will be put in his way by those who are perfectly well satisfied to go on as they are, in spite of the fact that a change is seen to be absolutely necessary in the long run.

In the following chapters we shall try to give a picture of how business and industry are conducted, and some explanation of the forces controlling each. Most of our business and industrial troubles arise from the fact that the controlling factors are not apparent to the public in general and can be disclosed only by a thorough and exhaustive study of what is taking place.

Following this general exposition of the subject, we shall show a system of progress charts which bear the same relation to the statistical reports which are so common that a moving picture film bears to a photograph. This chart system has been in use only a few years, but it is so simple that it is readily understood by the workman and employer, and so comprehensive that one intelligent workman made the remark, "If we chart everything we are doing that way, anybody can run the shop." While we are hardly prepared to agree with this opinion, we are entirely satisfied that if the facts about a business can be presented in a compact and comprehensive manner, it will be found possible to run any business much more effectively than has been the custom in the past.

We wish to emphasize the practicality of our methods, because we have been accused of preaching altruism in business, which our critics say will not work. We know altruism will not work and absolutely repudiate the idea that our methods are altruistic; as a matter of fact, we believe we should get full reward for service rendered. Moreover, we believe that if everybody got full reward for service rendered there would not be so many "profits" for the employer and employee to quarrel over, so often to the detriment of the public.

With this introduction, we shall try to make clear what has been happening in the industrial and business world, and draw our conclusions as we go along.

When the war broke out, many of our leading business men who had accumulated wealth through the accepted business methods, which had to do primarily with buying, selling, financing, etc., went to Washington and offered their services at a dollar a year. They did this with the best intentions, believing that the business methods which had brought them success in the past were the ones needed in time of war. They soon found that the government had taken over all financial operations; that there was no selling to be done, and that the problem quickly reduced itself to one of production, in which many of them had had no experience. There were, of course, many marked exceptions, for some grasped the problem at once and did wonderful work. As a general rule, however, this was not the case, for it takes a very capable man to grasp quickly the essentials of a big problem that is entirely new to him. Hence, as a rule, they adhered strictly to the methods they had been accustomed to, and called to assist them great numbers of accountants and statisticians (all static), both groups thoroughly convinced that record-keeping was the main aim of business; and while the army was calling for ships and shells, trucks and tanks, these men busied themselves with figures, piling up statistics, apparently quite satisfied that they were doing their part. In many cases these statisticians did not differentiate between that which is interesting and that which is important. In but few cases did they realize that from the standpoint of production, yesterday's record is valuable only as a guide for tomorrow. They did not understand that it is only the man who knows what to do and how to do it that can direct the accumulation of the facts he needs for his guidance. In too many cases, such men had been left behind to run the factories, while their superiors, who had had no experience in production, undertook for the government the most important job of production we have ever had, depending almost entirely upon accountants and statisticians for guidance. The results of their labors are now history, a knowledge of which will soon be the common property of all. In spite of this handicap, we did much good work.

There is no question that both our army and navy have made good to a degree which none of our allies anticipated, but it is also true that if we had not had economic assistance from our allies, the results they have obtained would have been impossible. As a matter of fact, it is well known that our industrial system has not measured up as we had expected. To substantiate this we have only to mention airplanes, ships, field guns, and shells. The reason for its falling short is undoubtedly that the men directing it had been trained in a business system operated for profits, and did not understand one operated solely for production. This is no criticism of the men as individuals; they simply did not know the job, and, what is worse, they did not know they did not know it.

Inasmuch as our economic strength in the future will be based on production, we must modify our system as rapidly as possible, with the end in view of putting producers in charge. To do this, opinions must give place to facts, and words to deeds, and the engineer, who is a man of few opinions and many facts, few words and many deeds, should be accorded the leadership which is his proper place in our economic system.

It must be remembered, however, that the engineer has two distinct functions. One is to design and build his machinery; the second is to operate it. In the past he has given more attention to the former function than to the latter. At first this was but a natural and necessary condition, for the various engineering structures were comparatively few and were operated in a measure simply and independently. Now, however, with the multiplicity of machines of all kinds, the operation of- one is many times intimately dependent upon the operation of another, even in one factory. In addition to this the operation of one factory is always dependent upon the successful operation of a number of others. Because this inter-operation is necessary to render service or produce results, the complexity of the operating problem has greatly increased, for the operation of a large number of factories in harmony presents much the same problem as the harmonious operation of the machines in one factory. It is only, however, where the factories have been combined under one management that any direct attempt at this kind of control has been made. To be sure, the relation between the demand for and supply of the product, supplemented by a desire to get the greatest possible profit, has resulted in a sort of control, which has usually been based more on opinion than facts, and generally exercised to secure the greatest possible profits rather than to render the greatest service.

Emphasizing again the self-evident fact that great reward can only be continuously got by corresponding service, and that the maximum service can be rendered only when actions are based on knowledge, we realize that the logical director for such work is the engineer, who not only has a basic knowledge of the work, but whose training and experience lead him to rely only upon facts. So far, however, there is not in general use any mechanism which will enable the engineer to visualize at once the large number of facts that must be comprehended in order that he may handle effectively the managerial problems that our modern industrial system is constantly presenting. It is one object of this book to lay before the public the progress we have made in visualizing the problems and the available information needed for their solution.

Chapter 3 - EFFICIENCY AND IDLENESS

WHAT we accomplished in our preparation for war and in getting men to the front surprised ourselves, and apparently satisfied our allies. It was accomplished by the splendid energy and tremendous resources of the American people, but nobody pretends that we showed any high degree of efficiency in doing the work. Our expenses were enormous, and we have reconciled ourselves to their magnitude by saying over and over again that nothing counted except wincing the war, which in the last analysis is true; but it is also true that excessive expense not only did not help us to win the war, but rather hindered us in accomplishing this result.

Our fumbling in war preparation seems to indicate that the great campaign for efficiency, which has been waged so assiduously in this country for the past twenty years, has not accomplished for us all we had led ourselves to believe. That we have increased individual efficiency and profit-making efficiency, and perhaps other kinds of efficiency, is not to be denied. That we have attained a high degree of national efficiency or a high degree of efficiency in the production of goods is nowhere indicated. It took the shock of a great war to arouse us to the realization that our great prosperity was due to something other than our productive efficiency.

Yet surely the long campaign for efficiency has been honestly and seriously waged. Why, then, have our results been so meager? The answer is simple enough and plain. The aim of our efficiency has not been to produce goods, but to harvest dollars. If we could harvest more dollars by producing fewer goods, we produced the fewer goods. If it happened that we could harvest more dollars by producing more goods, we made an attempt to produce more goods: but the production of goods was always secondary to the securing of dollars.

In the great emergency created by the war, our need was not for dollars but for goods, and people who had been trained for the seeking' of dollars were in most cases not at all fitted for the producing of goods. Those who had been most successful in acquiring dollars were, however, the ones best known as business men, and when it was thought we needed a business administration, such people, with the best intentions in the world, offered their services to the Federal Government, many at a great sacrifice of their own interests. They found, however, that for war we needed goods, and that dollars were only the means to that end. Then they found that unless people knew how to produce the goods, dollars were ineffective.

Another phase of the efficiency movement with which we are all so familiar, was the attempt to increase the efficiency of the worker, and to ignore entirely the idler, because the system of cost-keeping generally in vogue made that seem the most profitable thing to do. The case was worse than this, for not only did the system ignore the idler, but it eliminated the inefficient, absolutely ignoring the fact that both the inefficient and the idle were going to continue to live and be supported, directly or indirectly, by the workers.

The war waked us up to the fact that the world was running short of the necessities of life, and that the product of even the most inefficient was some help. The scheme for the selection of the efficient, of which much had been made, was now found to need supplementing by one for forcing the idler to work and training the inefficient.

The great difficulty of installing such a system was that the cost-keeping methods in general vogue indicated that training methods were not profitable, for trainers were classed as non- producers. In spite of this fact, however, the war emergency forced ns to adopt them, and the results were beneficial. The inevitable deduction is that the cost-keeping methods in general vogue are fundamentally wrong, and that we shall continue to suffer from inefficiency until they are corrected. The great error in them is the fact that they absolutely ignore the expense of idleness. As a matter of fact, it costs almost as much to be idle as it does to work. This is true whether we consider *men* or *machines, or, in other words, labor* or *capital.*

This leads us at once to two natural questions:

"What is our expense for idle labor?"

"What is our expense for idle capital?"

Manufacturing concerns pretty generally eliminate idle labor as completely as they can (many times by discharging workmen who could be profitably used if work were planned for them).

They cannot get rid of idle capital so easily, for it is tied up in machines that cannot be sold. The only possible way to eliminate idle capital, then, is to put it to work. The first step toward putting it to work is to find out why it is idle. As soon as this is done, means for putting it to work begin to suggest themselves. Our cost-keeping system, to meet the present and future emergency, must not content itself with charging to the product all expenses, but must charge to the product only that expense that helped to produce it, and must show the expenses that did not produce anything, and their causes. If this fundamental change is made in our cost-keeping methods, our viewpoint on the subject of production changes, with the result that we devote our attention first to the elimination of idleness, both of capital and labor.

Chapter 4 - PRODUCTION AND COSTS

MANUFACTURERS in general recognize the vital importance of knowledge of the cost of their product, yet but few of them have a cost system on which they are willing to rely under all conditions.

While it is possible to get quite accurately the amount of material and labor used directly in the production of an article, and several systems have been devised which accomplish this result, there does not yet seem to be in general use any system of distributing that portion of the expense known variously as indirect expense, burden, or overhead, in such a manner as to make us have any real confidence that it has been done properly.

There are in common use several methods of distributing this expense. One is to distribute to the product the total indirect expense, including interest, taxes, insurance, etc., according to the direct labor. Another is to distribute a portion of this expense according to direct labor, and a portion to machine hours. Other methods distribute a certain amount of this expense on the material used, etc. Most of these methods contemplate the distribution of all of the indirect expense of the manufacturing plant, however much it may be, on the output produced, no matter how small it is.

If the factory is running at its full, or normal, capacity, this item of indirect expense per unit of product is usually small. If the factory is running at only a fraction of its capacity, say one-half, and turning out only one-half of its normal product, there is but little change in the total amount of this indirect expense, all of which must now be distributed over half as much product as previously, each unit of product thereby being obliged to bear approximately twice as much expense as previously.

When times are good, and there is plenty of business, this method of accounting indicates that our costs are low; but when times become bad and business is slack, it indicates high costs due to the increased proportion of burden each unit has to bear. During good times, when there is a demand for the entire product we can make, it is usually sold at a high price and the element of cost is not such an important factor. When business is dull, however, we cannot get such a high price for our product, and the question of at how low a price we can afford to sell the product is of vital importance. Our cost systems, as generally operated at present, show under such conditions that our costs are high and, if business is very bad, they usually show us a cost far greater than the amount we can get for the goods. In other words, our present systems of cost accounting go to pieces when they are most needed. This being the case, many have felt for a long time that there was something radically wrong with the present theories on the subject.

As an illustration, I may cite a case which recently came to my attention. A man found that his cost on a certain article was thirty cents. When he found that he could buy it for twenty-six cents, he gave orders to stop manufacturing and to buy it, saying he did not understand how his competitor could sell at that price. He seemed to realize that there was a flaw somewhere, but he could not locate it. I asked him of what his expense consisted. His reply was, labor ten cents, material eight cents, and overhead twelve cents. I then asked if he was running his factory at full capacity, and got the reply that he was running it at less than half its capacity, possibly at one-third. The next question was: What would be the overhead on this article if the factory were running full?

The reply was that it would be about five cents. I suggested that in such a case the cost would be only twenty-three cents. The possibility that his competitor was running his factory full suggested itself at once as an explanation.

The next question that suggested itself was how the twelve cents overhead, which was charged to this article, would be paid if the article was bought. The obvious answer was that it would have to be distributed over the product still being made, and would thereby increase its cost. In such a case it would probably be found that some other article' was costing more than it could be bought for; and, if the same policy were pursued, the second article should be bought, which would cause the remaining product to bear a still higher expense rate. If this policy were carried to its logical conclusion, the manufacturer would be buying everything before long, and be obliged to give up manufacturing entirely.

The illustration which I have cited is not an isolated case, but is representative of the problems before a large class of manufacturers, who believe that all of the expense, however large, must be carried by the output produced, however small. This theory of expense distribution indicates a policy which in dull times would, if followed logically, put many manufacturers out of business. In 1897 the plant of which I was superintendent was put out of business by just this kind of logic. It never started up again.

Fortunately for the country, American people as a whole will finally discard theories which conflict with common sense; and, when their cost figures indicate an absurd conclusion, most of them will repudiate the figures. A cost system, however, which fails us when we need it most, is of but little value and it is imperative for us to devise a theory of costs that will not fail us.

Most of the cost systems in use, and the theories on which they are based, have been devised by accountants for the benefit of financiers, whose aim has been to criticize the factory and to make it responsible for all the shortcomings of the business. In this they have succeeded admirably, largely because the methods used are not so devised as to enable the superintendent to present his side of the case.

One of the prime functions of cost-keeping is to enable the superintendent to know whether or not he is doing the work he is responsible for as economically as possible, a function which **is** ignored in the majority of cost systems now in general use. Many accountants who make attempt to show it, are so long in getting their figures in shape that they are practically worthless for the purpose intended, the possibility of using them having passed.

In order to get a correct view of the subject we must look at the matter from a different and broader standpoint. The following illustration may put the subject in its true light:

Let us suppose that a manufacturer owns three identical plants, of an economical operating size, manufacturing the same article,—one located in Albany, one in Buffalo, and one in Chicago—and that they arc all running at their normal capacity and are managed equally well. The amount of indirect expense per unit of product would be substantially the same in each of these factories, as would be the total cost. Now suppose business suddenly falls off to one-third of its previous amount and the manufacturer shuts down the plants in Albany and Buffalo, and continues to run the one in Chicago exactly as it has been run before. The product from the Chicago plant would have the same cost that it previously had, but the expense of carrying two idle factories might be so great as to take all the profits out of the business; in other words, the profit made from the Chicago plant might be offset entirely by the loss made by the Albany and Buffalo plants.

If these plants, instead of being in different cities, were located in the same city, a similar condition might also exist in which the expense of the two idle plants would be such a drain on the business that they would offset the profit made in the going plant.

Instead of considering these three factories to be in different parts of one city, they might be considered as being within the same yard, which would not change the conditions. Finally, we might consider that the walls between these factories were taken down and that the three factories were turned into one plant, the output of which had been reduced to one-third of its normal volume. In such case it would be manifestly proper to charge to this product only one-third of the indirect expense charged when the factory was running full.

If the above argument is correct, we may state the following general principle: THE IN-DIRECT EXPENSE CHARGEABLE TO THE OUTPUT OF A FACTORY SHOULD BEAR THE SAME RATIO TO THE INDIRECT EXPENSE NECESSARY TO RUN THE FACTORY AT NORMAL CAPACITY, AS THE OUTPUT IN QUESTION BEARS TO THE NORMAL OUTPUT OF THE FACTORY.

This theory of expense distribution, which was forced upon us by the abrupt change in conditions brought on by the war, explains many things which were inexplicable under the older theory, and gives the manufacturer uniform, or at least comparable, costs as long as the methods of manufacture do not change.

Under this method of distributing expense there will be a certain amount of undistributed expense remaining whenever the factory runs below its normal capacity. A careful consideration of this item will show that it is not chargeable to the product made, but is a business expense incurred on account of maintaining a certain portion of the factory idle, and chargeable to profit and loss. Many manufacturers have made money in a small plant, then built a large plant and lost money for years afterward, without quite understanding how it happened. This method of figuring affords an explanation and warns the manufacturer to do everything possible to increase the efficiency of the plant he has, rather than to increase its size.

This theory explains why some of our large combinations of manufacturing plants have not been as successful as was anticipated, and why the small plant is able to compete successfully and make money, while the combinations are only just holding their own.

The idea so prevalent a few years ago, that in the industrial world money is the most powerful factor, and that if we only had enough money, nothing- else would matter very much, is beginning to lose its force, for it is becoming clear that the size of a business is not so important as the policy by which it is directed. If we base our policy on the idea that the cost of an article can only legitimately include the expense necessarily incurred either directly or indirectly in producing it, we shall find that our costs are much lower than we thought, and that we can do many things which under the old method of figuring appeared suicidal.

The view of costs so largely held, namely, that the product of a factory, however small, must bear the total expense, however large, is responsible for much of the confusion about costs and hence leads to unsound business policies.

If we accept the view that the article produced shall bear only that portion of the indirect expense needed to produce it, our costs will not only become lower, but relatively far more constant, for the most variable factor in the cost of an article under the usual system of accounting has been the "overhead," which has varied almost inversely as the amount of the product. This item becomes substantially constant if the "overhead" is figured on the normal capacity of the plant.

Of course a method of cost-keeping does not diminish the expense, but it may show where the expense properly belongs, and give a more correct understanding of the business.

In our illustration of the three factories, the cost in the Chicago factory remained constant, but the expense of supporting the Buffalo and Albany factories in idleness was a charge against the business, and properly chargeable to profit and loss. If we had loaded this expense on the product of the Chicago factory, the cost of the product would probably have been so great as to have prevented our selling it, and the total loss would have been greater still.

When the factories are distinctly separate, few people make such a mistake, but where a single factory is three times as large as is needed for the output, the error is frequently made, with results that are just as misleading.

As a matter of fact it seems that the attempt to make a product bear the expense of plant not needed for its production is one of the most serious defects in our industrial system today, and farther reaching than the differences between employers and employees, for if it were removed, most of the difficulties would vanish.

The problem that faces us is first to find just what plant or part of a plant is needed to produce a given output, and then to determine the "overhead" expense needed to operate that plant or portion of that plant. This is primarily the work of the manufacturer, or engineer, and only secondarily that of the accountant, who must, as far as costs are concerned, be the servant of the superintendent.

In the past, in almost all cost systems the amount of "overhead" to be charged to the product, when it did not include all the "overhead," was more or less a matter of judgment. According to the theory now presented, it is not a matter of judgment, but can be determined with an accuracy depending upon the knowledge the manufacturer has of the business. Following this line of thought it should be possible for a manufacturer to calculate just what plant and equipment he ought to have, and what the staff of officers and workmen should be to turn out a given product. If this can be correctly done, the exact cost of a product can be predicted. Such a problem cannot be solved by a cost accountant without shop knowledge, but is primarily a problem for an engineer whose knowledge of materials and processes is essential for its solution.

In any attempt to solve a problem of this type, one of the most important functions we need a cost system to perform is to keep the superintendent continually advised as to how nearly he is realizing the ideal set, and to point out where the shortcomings are.

Many of us are accustomed to this viewpoint when we are treating operations singly, but few have as yet made an attempt to consider that this idea might be applied to a plant as a whole, except when the processes of manufacture are simple and the products few in number. When, however, the processes become numerous or complicated, the necessity for such a cheek becomes more urgent, and the cost-keeper who performs this function becomes an integral part of the manufacturing system, and acts for the superintendent, as an inspector, who keeps him advised at all times of the quality of his own work.

This conception of the duties of a cost-keeper does not at all interfere with his supplying the financier with the information he needs, but insures that the information shall be correct, for the cost-keeper is continually making a comparison for the benefit of the superintendent, of what has been done with what should have been done. Costs are valuable only as comparisons, and comparisons are of little value unless we have a standard, which it is the function of the engineer to set.

Lack of reliable cost methods has, in the past, been responsible for much of the uncertainty so prevalent in our industrial policies; but with a definite and reliable cost method, which enables us to differentiate between what is lost in manufacturing and what is lost in business, it will usually become easy to define clearly the proper business policy.

Chapter 5 - VALUE OF AN INDUSTRIAL PROPERTY
DEPENDS ON ITS PRODUCTIVE CAPACITY

IN the summer of 1916 a professor of political economy in one of our most conservative universities admitted to me that the economists had been obliged to modify many of their views since the outbreak of the European war. My comment was that the professors of political economy were not the only people who had been obliged to modify their economic and industrial views.

The war taught everybody something. Military methods have undergone radical changes, but industrial methods are undergoing changes which promise to be even more radical than the military developments have been.

If there is any one thing which has been made clear by the war it is, that the most important asset which either a man or nation can have is the ABILITY TO DO THINGS. Our industrial and economic developments have in the past been largely based on the theory that the most important quality a man can possess is his ability to buy things; but the war has distinctly shown that this quality is secondary to the ability to do things. The recognition of this fact is having a most far-reaching effect, for it makes clear that the real assets of a nation are properly equipped industries and men trained to operate them efficiently. The money which has been spent on an industrial property, whether it has been spent wisely or unwisely, and the amount of money needed to reproduce it are both secondary in importance to the ability of that plant to accomplish the object for which it was constructed, and hence cannot be given the first place in determining the value of the property.

Inasmuch as every industrial plant is built to produce some article of commerce at a cost which will enable it to compete with other producers, the value of a plant as a producing unit must depend upon its ability to accomplish the object for which it was created.

To determine the value of an industrial property, therefore, we must be able to know with accuracy the cost at which it can produce its product, and the amount it can produce. . To compare two factories on this basis, their cost systems must be alike; for, if there is a lack of agreement as to methods of cost accounting there will necessarily be a lack of agreement as to the estimated value of the properties. There are many methods of cost accounting; but there are only two leading theories as to what cost consists of. They are:

First, that the cost of an article must include all the expense incurred in producing it, whether such expense actually contributed to the desired end or not.

Second, that the cost of an article should include only those expenses actually needed for its production, and any other expenses incurred by the producers for any reason whatever must be charged to some other account.

The first theory would charge the expense of maintaining in idleness that portion of a. plant which was not in use to the cost of the product made in that portion of the plant which was in operation; while the second theory would demand that such an expense be a deduction from profits, or at least be charged to some other account. When plants are operated at their full capacity, both theories give the same cost. If, however, they are operated at less than their full capacity, the expense of carrying the idle machinery is, under the first theory, included in the cost of the product, making the cost greater; while under the second theory, this expense of idle 'machinery is carried in a separate account and should be deducted from the profits, leaving the cost constant, It is most interesting to note that, when costs are figured on the second basis, great activity immediately ensues to determine why machinery is idle, and to see what can be done to put it in operation. It is realized at once that this machinery had better be operated, even if no profits are obtained from its operation and only the expense, or even part of the expense, of owning and maintaining it is earned.

Fig. 1 illustrates this subject most clearly, and is an indication of the efficiency of the management as contrasted with that of the workmen, about which we hear so much. It is interesting to note that charts of this nature, which are being made monthly in several large plants, have already had a very educational influence on the managers of those plants. They show that idle machinery which cannot be used, should be disposed of, the money received, the space occupied, and put to some useful purpose.

Figure 1

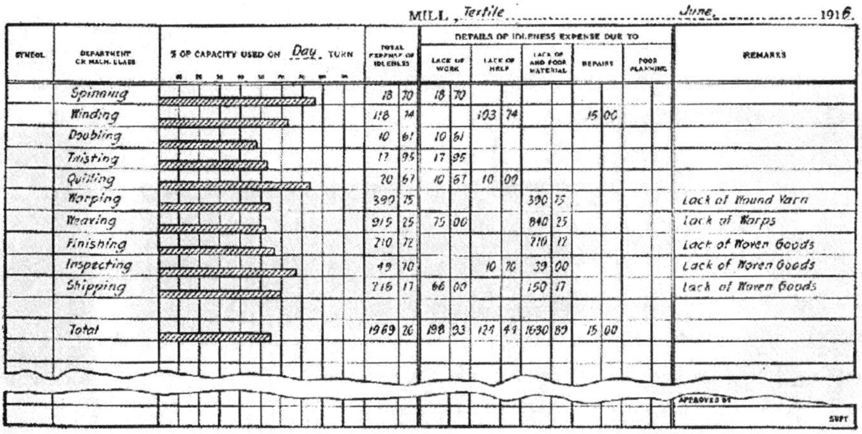

MILL, _Textile_ .... _June_ .... 1916.

SYMBOL	DEPARTMENT OR MACH. CLASS	% OF CAPACITY USED ON _Day_. TURN	TOTAL EXPENSE OF IDLENESS	DETAILS OF IDLENESS EXPENSE DUE TO					REMARKS
				LACK OF WORK	LACK OF HELP	LACK OF AND POOR MATERIAL	REPAIRS	POOR PLANNING	
	Spinning		18 70	18 70					
	Winding		118 74		103 74		15 00		
	Doubling		10 61	10 61					
	Twisting		17 95	17 95					
	Quilting		20 67	10 67	10 00				
	Warping		390 75			390 75			Lack of Wound Yarn
	Weaving		915 25	75 00		840 25			Lack of Warps
	Finishing		210 12			210 12			Lack of Woven Goods
	Inspecting		49 70		10 70	39 00			Lack of Woven Goods
	Shipping		216 17	66 00		150 17			Lack of Woven Goods
	Total		1969 26	198 93	124 44	1630 89	15 00		

| | | | | | | | | | | APPROVED BY | |
| | | | | | | | | | | | SUPT |

FIG. 1.—IDLENESS EXPENSE CHART

A little consideration of the method of getting the data on this chart will make its value more apparent. It is a logical outgrowth of the previous chapter on Production and Costs, and is based on the fact that simple ownership of a machine costs money, inasmuch as it takes away from available assets. For instance, if we buy a machine for $1,000 we lose the interest on that $1,000, say at five per cent per year, then we have taxes on the machine at two per cent, and insurance of one per cent. Further, the machine probably depreciates at a rate of twenty per cent per year, and we must pay $50 or more per year for the rent of the space it occupies. All these expenses, together $330, go on whether we use the machine or not. Thus, the simple fact of our having bought this machine and kept it takes from our available assets approximately one dollar per day.

If now the cause for idleness is ascertained each day we can find the expense of each cause of idleness as shown on the chart. That part which is due to lack of orders points out that our selling policy is wrong, or that the plant is larger than it should be-in other words, that somebody in building the plant has overestimated the demand. It is clear, however, that no conclusion should be based on the figures for one month, but on the results for a series of months during which the problem has been carefully studied. If a mistake has been made in building too large a plant, an effort should be made, to determine the proper disposal, or utilization, of the excess, in order that the expense of idleness may be taken care of, even if no profit can be made.

The next column shows the expense due to a lack of help, which means that we must investigate the labor policy.

The next column, showing the expense due to lack of, or poor, material, is an indication of the efficiency of the purchasing policy and storekeeping system. The next column reflects the repair and maintenance department.

104

If in any case the expense of idleness is greater than can be attributed to all of these causes together, it must go in the last column as poor planning.

We can hardly claim that such a chart gives us a measure of the efficiency with which the above functions are performed, but it certainly does give us an indication of that efficiency. In .several cases, the first of such charts gotten out resulted in the scrapping of machinery which had been idle for years. The space thus saved was used for a purpose for which the superintendent had felt he needed a new building. In another case it resulted in the renting of temporarily idle machinery at a rate which went far toward covering the expense of carrying that machinery.

Under the first system of cost-keeping the facts brought out by this method are not available and the increased cost that a reduced output must bear is a great source of confusion to the salesman. The newer system with its constant cost shows that non-producing machinery is a handicap to the industry of a company, just as workmen who do not serve some useful purpose in a plant, or industry, are a handicap to that plant or industry. Similarly, plants or people, therefore, who do not serve some useful purpose to a community are a handicap to that community, for idle plants represent idle capital, and idle people are not producers but consumers only. The warring nations recognized these facts, and put both idle plants and idle people to work wherever possible.

The statements so far made concern principally the operation of industrial plants and the production of articles of commerce; but they are none the less true concerning the construction of industrial plants. We may ask the same question about construction that we ask about operation; for instance, should the" cost" of a railroad include all the money spent by the people engaged in building it, or should it include only such money as contributed to the building of the road? As an illustration, is the cost of a piece of road which was built and then abandoned for a superior route before being used a part of the cost of the railroad built, or is it an expense due to improper judgment on the part of the builders.

I am not discussing the question as to whether the public should be called upon to pay interest on the money uselessly spent through improper judgment, but I do think that in. all construction it should be possible to separate those expenses which contributed to the desired result from those which did not so contribute. A comparison of these amounts will give a measure of the efficiency of the builders. On this knowledge, proper action can ultimately be taken.

Still another factor enters into the value of a "going plant, we all have known cases where the same plant operated under one manager was a failure, and under another a very decided success. The value of a going plant, therefore, consists of two elements; namely, the value of the physical real estate and equipment, and the value of the organization operating it. In considering the value of an organization we should realize that it lies not so much in the personality of the managers or leaders (who may die or go elsewhere) as is, the permanent results of their training and methods, which should go on with the business, and are therefore an asset and not an accident.

We have the authority of no less a person than Andrew Carnegie, for the statement that his organizations were of more value to him than his plants. Before we can determine exactly the value of a going plant, therefore, we must find some means of measuring the value of the organization which operates it, for this is an integral factor in the valuation of an industrial property, which is just as real as the more tangible brick and mortar of which buildings are composed.

Our charts showing the expense of idleness give us at least a rough indication of this value, for they show the expense of inefficient management.

Chapter 6 - AN EXTENSION OF THE CREDIT SYSTEM TO MAKE IT DEMOCRATIC

LOOKING backward over the great war, we have the opportunity better to understand and evaluate the different phenomena which were developed by it. Many incidents which seemed natural and in a measure unimportant when they took place, had a profound effect upon the outcome of the war, and promise to affect still more profoundly the period to follow.

Perhaps no one incident was more significant and fraught with greater consequences to the civilization of the world than the transfer, soon after we entered the war, of the credit center from Wall Street to Washington. This transfer took place without creating any stir, without any special opposition, and with the general approval of the community at large. We had' just got the Federal Reserve Banking System into operation, and it had enormously increased our power as a nation to dispense credit, yet notwithstanding the most advantageous position in which we had thus been placed, the expert financiers of Wall Street submitted without remonstrance to the transfer of the whole credit center to Washington, where it was administered by men who, compared with the "giants" of Wall Street, were mere amateurs.

Why was it necessary for this transfer to be made, and why did Wall Street consent to it? Surely if it had been within the possibilities of Wall Street to finance the war, a serious remonstrance at least would have been raised to this transfer of the credit center. The New York bankers not only did not remonstrate, but in a most patriotic manner offered their services to help the comparatively inexperienced men in Washington handle their great undertaking.

If it had been possible for Wall Street to finance the war, it is inconceivable that the bankers of New York should have allowed the work to be taken over by other hands. Why, then, was it possible for Washington to do what was impossible for Wall Street The answer to this question is not only very simple, but is indicative of the flaw in our whole business system. The financial methods of Wall Street were designed to operate only when we conducted "business as usual;" hence their mechanism could give credit only to those who had tangible securities. They had no mechanism for extending credit to men who, although they had few or no tangible assets, might have tremendous productive capacity.

Because the war demanded that the nations as a whole produce goods to the utmost, we were obliged to invent a new kind of finance, in which the production of goods would be the first object. There was no tradition among the bankers of this country for financing any proposition except on the basis of tangible assets, and for the sole purpose of making profits.

In many cases men who knew how to build ships or to make guns did not have tangible assets in sufficient quantity to satisfy the usual banking system. It was therefore necessary for the Federal Government to initiate a finance which was new, at least in this country: namely, that of extending credit to a man according to his productive capacity. There was no established mechanism for doing this, but it had to be done, and we did it, in a rather haphazard and ineffective manner. Nevertheless, the results have justified the venture, and the possibilities of a new credit system of vastly greater potentiality are opening themselves to us as soon as the mechanism for its operation shall have been developed.

A few of the great leaders of industry have understood In a general way this kind of finance. Among them may be mentioned Mr. Andrew Carnegie, who said he valued his organization more than his plants; and Mr. Henry Ford, Mr. Carnegie, through an understanding of this general principle, was able to dominate the steel industry; and Mr. Ford, by the same token, became the greatest automobile manufacturer in the world. The war has backed up Mr. Carnegie and Mr. Ford by proving that productive capacity is enormously more important than wealth, but inasmuch as our credit system has been based on "tangible assets," and not on productive capacity, there has been developed as yet no generally accepted mechanism for measuring the value of productive capacity.

The cost and accounting systems in general vogue take note only of what are called the "tangible assets," which are necessarily static, showing only potentialities. They make but little attempt to find out how these assets are being used. The reason undoubtedly is that they see such assets from a sales standpoint; in other words, our economic system is still patterned after the one which was originally built up to serve the needs of buying and selling. Productive capacity, on the other hand, can be measured only by taking account of what is happening. When we begin to regard matters from this standpoint, the so-called "tangible assets" are not nearly so important as the use being made of them, or the amount of product being turned out. In other words, the modern accounting system which deals with production must give us it picture of what is happening, as well as of the mechanism which causes the happenings. It must be based on charts which show what progress is taking place, and which bear the same relation to statistics as a moving picture film does to a photograph.

The question naturally asked is: If the above statements are correct, why have we not realized their correctness before? It took a great war, which required us to put forth all our strength, to wake us up to their importance. They have been increasing in importance for a number of years, and our failure to recognize this fact was one of the factors in producing the great catastrophe through which we have just passed.

For many years previous to the outbreak of the great war, financiers told us there couldn't be any war, because the bankers wouldn't stand for it. They thought money controlled the world. Books were written to prove that we could have no more war. The idea of war was called "the great illusion." When this "illusion" was realized, they still maintained that the war could last only a few months. Nevertheless it lasted over four years, to the great confusion of our economists and theorists. We all know now that it was supported, not by finance, but by the grand scale production of modern industry. It stopped, not for lack of money, but for lack of means to live and fight with. We see, then, without any possible shadow of doubt, that inasmuch as production was the controlling factor in the great war, it will hereafter be the controlling factor in the world, and that nation which first recognizes the fundamental fact that production, and not money, must be the aim of our economic system, will, other things being equal, exert a predominating influence on the civilization, which is to be built up in the period of reconstruction upon which we are now entering.

Our immediate problem, then, is to develop a credit system that will enable us to take advantage of all the productive forces in the community. Such a credit system must not only be able to finance those who have ownership, but also those who have productive capacity, which is vastly more important. This is equivalent to saying that our wealth in men is more important than our wealth in materials. So far we have never used this force to more than a small fraction of its capacity, simply for the reason, as previously stated, that the originators of our financial system were traders and not producers. Now, however, when the supreme importance of the producer has been recognized, we must enlarge our credit system in such a manner as to enable us to take full advantage of his possibilities; in other words, we must make it democratic.

To meet the exigencies of war the Federal Government had no hesitation in inaugurating such finance, for the benefit of the community.

While it was done in a new and crude manner, we recognize that it was in the main successful. We shall soon find that there are exigencies in times of peace also that could be helped by a similar financial method. Some nations are going to see this, and realizing that the credit system of the country must always be available for the benefit of the community, take such action as to accomplish that result, and thereby force others to do the same. Through the War Finance Corporation Act (amended) section 21, March 3, 1919, we have already taken such action with regard to exports. During the war, we financed necessary production with public money; now in time of peace we finance another essential activity with public money" This is a most encouraging beginning. Can we not make public money available for the financing of all socially necessary activities whether of war or peace?

In the past what a man could do was limited by his financial and social condition; hence many of our most capable men were severely restricted in their activities. To be sure, a few have been able to rise above their restrictions -a rail splitter becomes the president of a great republic, and a harness-maker the first president of another. These examples, however, only illustrate the possibilities that are unutilized, because our credit system has not been democratic.

Chapter 7 - ECONOMICS OF DEMOCRACY

THE prime function of a science is to enable us to anticipate the future in the field with which it has to deal. Judged by this standard, economic science has in the past been practically worthless; for it absolutely failed to warn us of the greatest catastrophe that has ever befallen the civilized world. Further, when the catastrophe burst upon us, economists and financiers persisted in belittling it by insisting that the Great War could last only a few months. Are they any nearer the truth in their theories of labor and capital, protection and free trade, or taxation?

When they talk about preparedness, what do they mean? *Do they mean that we must so order our living as to prevent another such catastrophe, or do they simply mean that we must aim to be strong when the next catastrophe comes?*

The latest economic thought indicates clearly that the fundamentals of both kinds of preparedness are the same, and that preparation for the former is the best basis on which to establish preparation for the latter. *True preparedness, then, would seem to consist in a readjustment of our economic conditions with the object of averting another such catastrophe.*

In considering this subject we must realize that:

The Nation reflects its leaders.

The Army reflects its general.

The Factory reflects its manager.

In a successful industrial nation, the industrial leaders must ultimately become the leaders of the nation. The condition of the in-dustries will then become a true index of the condition of the nation. If the industries are not properly managed for the benefit of the whole community, no amount of *military* preparedness will avail in a *real* war. The military preparations of Germany, vast as they were, would have collapsed in six months had it not been for the social and industrial conditions on which they were based.

Army officers and others have told us most emphatically what military preparedness is, and how to get it. Innumerable papers have been written on industrial preparedness, and people in general are getting a pretty clear idea of what we mean by the term. Moreover, many are beginning to appreciate our lack in this respect. Figs. 2, 3, 4, and 5 illustrate what this means.

Admittedly these pictures are not typical of our industries, but they do represent a condition which is all too common, and which must be corrected if we are to be prepared either for peace or for war.

Our record in the production of munitions, especially of ammunition, is not one to be proud of. Note what Mr. Bascom Little, President of the Cleveland, Ohio, Chamber of Commerce, and Chairman of the National Defense Committee of the Chamber of Commerce of the United States, said in the spring of 1916:

"The work of Mr. Coffin's committee has seemed to us very important, and so clearly related, in such practical ways, to what the business organizations of the country are trying to do to further national defense, that those with which I am connected immediately formed a union with the committee on learning of its work.

"The thing that has stirred up the business men of the Middle West during the past eighteen months has been the lesson they have learned in the making of war materials. It points a very vivid moral to all our people. It all looked very easy when it started a year and a half ago. The plant with which I am associated in Cleveland got an order for 250,000 three-inch high explosive shells. It was a simple enough looking job-just a question of machining.

Figure 2

FIG. 2.—UNPREPARED

Fig. 3.—Prepared

Two views of the same shop doing substantially the same work. The lower picture was taken about a year after the upper from a slightly different viewpoint.

Figure 3

The forgings were shipped to us and we were to finish and deliver. It began to dawn on us when the forgings came that this whole order, that looked so big to us, was less than one day's supply of shells for France or England or Russia; and we felt that in eight months by turning our plant, which is a first-class machine shop, onto this job we could fill the order. In a little while we got up against the process of hardening. That-and mark what I say -was fourteen months ago. To date we have shipped and had accepted *130,000* shells, and those, about half our order, are not complete. They still have to be fitted by the fuse maker, then fitted in the brass cartridge cases with the propelling charge, and somewhere, sometime, maybe, they will get on the battle-field of Europe. Up to the present, none of them has arrived there.

"Now this is the situation in a high-class efficient American plant. This is what happened when it turned to making munitions of war. The same thing has occurred in so many Middle Western plants, that their owners have made up their minds that if they are ever going to be called upon for service to their own country, they must know more about this business. They feel that they are now liabilities to the nation and not assets in case of war. *Proud as we may be of our industrial perfection, it has not worked here, and the country-particularly you in the East -may as well know it."*

The comment on this will be that it is three years old, and that we have made great advances since then. In reply I can only say that if we have made marked advances I have been utterly unable to discover them.

The most casual investigation into the reasons why so many of the munitions manufacturers have not made good, reveals the fact that *their failure is due to lack of managerial ability* rather than to any other cause. Without efficiency in management, efficiency of the workmen is useless, even if it is possible to get it. With an efficient management there -is but little difficulty in training the workmen to be efficient. I have proved this so many times and so clearly that there can be absolutely no doubt about it. Our most serious trouble is incompetence in high places. As long as that remains uncorrected, no amount of efficiency in the workmen will avail very much.

The pictures by which this chapter is illustrated do not show anything concerning the efficiency of the individual workman, but they are a sweeping condemnation of the inefficiency of those responsible for the management, mid illustrate the fact, so well known to many of us, that our industries are suffering from lack of competent managers, which is another way of saying that many of those who control our industries hold their positions, not through their ability to accomplish results, but for some other reason. In other words, industrial control is too often based on favoritism or privilege, rather than on ability. *This hampers the healthy, normal development of industrialism, which can reach its highest development only when equal opportunity is secured to all, and when all reward is equitably proportioned to service rendered. In other words, when industry becomes democratic.*

We are, therefore, brought face to face with a form of preparedness which is even more fundamental than the Industrial Preparedness usually referred to, and I am indebted to Mr. W. N. Polakov for the name" Social Preparedness," which means the democratization of industry and the establishment of such relations among the citizens themselves, and between the citizens and the government, as will cause a hearty and spontaneous response on the part of the citizens to the needs of the country.

Figure 4

FIG. 4.—UNPREPARED

Figure 5

FIG. 4.—UNPREPARED

FIG. 5.—PREPARED

Two views of the same shop doing substantially the same work, taken from the same point. The lower view was taken about a year after the upper.

At the breaking out of the Great War in Europe, the thing which perhaps surprised us most was the enthusiasm with which the German people entered into it. Hardly less striking was the slowness with which the rank and file of Englishmen realized the problems they were up against, and their responsibilities concerning them.

A short consideration of what happened in Germany in the last half of the nineteenth century, or before the war, may throw some light on this subject. Bismarck and Von Moltke, following the lead of Frederick the Great, believed and taught that the great industry of a country was war. In other words, that it was more profitable to take by violence from another than to produce. The history of the world, *until the development of modern industrialism,* seemed to bear out that theory. Bismarck argued that to be strong from a military standpoint the nation must have a large number of well trained, intelligent, healthy men, and he set about so ordering the industries of Germany as to produce that result.

Military autocracy forced business and industry to see that men were properly trained and that their health was safe-guarded. In other words, because of the necessity of the military state for such men, the state saw to it that industry was so organized as to develop high-grade men, with the result that a kind of industrial democracy was developed under the paternalistic guidance of an autocratic military party.

Under such influences, the increase of education and the development of men went on apace, and were soon reflected in an industrial system which bade fair to surpass any other in the world.

In England, on the other hand, the business system was controlled by an autocratic and "socially irresponsible finance," which, to a large extent, disregarded the interest of the workman and of the community. At the breaking out of the war, the superiority of the industries of Germany over the industries of England was manifest, not only by the feeling of the people, but by their loyalty to the National Government, which had so cared for, or disregarded, their individual welfare. This superiority became so rapidly apparent, that in order to make any headway against Germany, England was obliged to imitate the methods which had been developed in Germany, and to say that *the industries* (particularly the munitions factories) *which were needed for the salvation of the country, must serve the country and not the individual.* The increased efficiency which England showed after the adoption of this method was most marked, and in striking contrast with the inefficiency displayed previously in similar work.

Confessedly our industries are not managed in the interest of the community, but in that of an autocratic finance. In Germany it was proved beyond doubt that an industrial system, forced by military autocracy to serve the community, is vastly stronger than an industrial system which serves only a financial autocracy.

The method by which Germany developed a singleness of purpose and tremendous power both for peace and for war-namely, autocratic military authority-is hateful to us, but we must not lose sight of the fact that such power *was developed* and may be developed by some other nation again in the future. If we would be strong when we are again faced with a contingency of developing a greater strength, or submitting, we must first of all develop a single~ ness of purpose for the whole community.

England demonstrated the same thing; for had England not rapidly increased her efficiency in the production of munitions, it would have been indeed a sad day for the British Empire.

In considering these facts, we should ask ourselves if there is not some fundamental fact which is accountable for the success of industry under such control. The one thing which stands out most prominently is the fact that, in the attempt to make the industries serve the community, *an attempt was made to abolish industrial privilege, and to give every man an opportunity to do what he could and to reward him correspondingly.*

As before stated, the industrial system of Germany was developed largely as an adjunct to its military system, .which, to a degree at least, forced the abolition of financial and industrial privilege, and thereby in a large measure eliminated in competency in high places. What results may not be expected, therefore, if we abolish privilege absolutely, and devote all our efforts to the development of an industrialism which shall serve the community and thus "develop the unconquerable power of real democracy?"

The close of the war and the abolition of political autocracy has brought us face to face with the question of a choice between the economic autocracy of the past, or an economic democracy. To prove that this is not mere idle speculation, note what one of our leading financiers said on the subject during the war:

"The President of the New York Life Insurance Company," says Mr. Charles Ferguson, "told the State Chamber of Commerce, during the great war, that under modern conditions the existence of even two rival sovereignties on this little planet has become absurd. This is true. We must therefore drive forward, through incredible waste and slaughter, to the settlement of the question of which of the rival Powers is to build the New Rome, and establish a military world-state on the Cresarean model - or else we must now set our faces toward a real democracy."

What is the basis of such a democracy?

The one thing in the entire civilized world, which, like the Catholic Church of the middle Ages, crosses all frontiers and binds together all peoples, is business. The Chinaman and the American by means of an interpreter find a common interest in business. Business is therefore the one possible bond which may bring universal peace. *Economists and financiers fully realized this, and believed that an autocratic finance could accomplish the result.* That was their fatal error. *The beneficiaries of privilege invariably battle among themselves, even if they are strong enough to hold in subjection those that have no privileges, and who have to bear the brunt of the fight.*

This is true whether the beneficiaries be individuals or nations, hence neither internal strife nor external war can be eliminated as long as some people have privileges over others.

If privilege be eliminated not only will the danger of war be minimized, but the causes of domestic strife will be much reduced in number. Then, and not until then, will the human race be in a position to make a continuous and' uninterrupted advance.

The nation which first realizes this fact and eliminates privilege from business will have a distinct lead on all others, and, other conditions being equal will rapidly rise to a dominating place in the world. Such a nation will do by means of the arts of peace, which some Germans seemed to think it was their mission to do by means of war. The opportunity is knocking at our door. Shall we turn it away?

The answer is that we must not turn it away.

In fact, we dare not, if we would escape the economic convulsion that is now spreading over Europe. Soon after the signing of the armistice Mr. David R. Francis, formerly ambassador to Russia, said that the object of the Soviet Government was to prevent the exploitation of one man by another. According to Mr. Francis, the cause of this convulsion is the attempt of the social body to free itself of the exploitation of one man by another. Then he added, "Such an aim is manifestly absurd". The convulsion is made all the more severe because there are people in every community that not only consider this aim absurd, but use all their influence to prevent the accomplishment of it.

If, at the end of a victorious war for democracy, a prominent representative of the victors is willing to proclaim publicly such a sentiment, it is perfectly evident that we have not yet solved all of our problems. Whether we approve of the Soviet method of government or not, even Mr. Francis must admit that their aim, as expressed by him, is a worthy one. It would be surprising if in the time which has elapsed since the Russian revolution an entirely satisfactory and permanent method should have been developed to prevent the exploitation of one man by another, but the fact that they have not yet established such a government is hardly a basis for the statement that the establishment of such a government is absurd.

This statement by Mr. Francis brings clearly to the front the question-Is our business system of the future going to continue to be one of exploitation of one man by another, or is it possible to have a business system from which such privilege has been eliminated?

In this connection it may be interesting to note that, for the past fifteen years, I and a small band of co-workers have been attempting to develop a system of industrial management which should not be dependent on the exploitation of one man by another, but should aim to give each as nearly as possible his just dues. Strange as it may seem to those of the old way of thinking, the more nearly successful we have been in this attempt, the more prosperous have the concerns adopting our methods be come. In view of this fact we beg to submit that the proposition does not seem to us to be absurd, even though we may not admit that any of the solutions heretofore offered have really accomplished the result. In a subsequent chapter, however, we shall present the progress which we have recently made in this direction.

Chapter 8 - DEMOCRACY IN PRODUCTION

(Progress Charts)

It is unquestionable that the strategy of General Foch, who so promptly took advantage of the error of the Germans in not flattening out the French salient between Montdidier and Chateau-Thierry, enabled him to establish his offensive which, with the new spirit put into his whole force by the splendid fresh troops of the American army, would undoubtedly have wrested victory from the Germans in the long run, even if they had been able to stave off the revolution at home and keep their economic system in good shape. It is a fact, however, that a growing discontent due to the increasing hardships which their economic system was unable to relieve, and which threatened a revolution, was unquestionably an important factor in lowering the morale of the army and worked strongly in our favor. Of course, knowledge of the real conditions at home was kept as much as possible from the soldiers at the front, but from what we have learned since the armistice it must have been perfectly clear to those in control some time before the armistice, that their economic strength was exhausted, and hence, the end had come.

It has even been suggested that the attempt of the Germans to extend the salient at Chateau-Thierry before they flattened out the salient between Montdidier and that point, was taking a "gambler's chance," for they realized then that they were near the end of their economic resources and that they must have a quick victory or none.

Whether this theory is true or not, the fact remains that the threatened collapse of the economic system was a controlling factor during the last few months of the war. In other words, war cannot be waged unless the economic system is capable of supporting the population and also furnishing the fighting equipment. To be as strong as possible in war, therefore, we must develop an economic system which will enable us to exert all our strength for the common good, which will therefore be free from autocratic practices of either rich or poor, for such practices take away from the community for the benefit of a class.

It is pretty generally agreed that this philosophy is correct in time of war, but both the rich and the poor seem to think that we do not need to be strong in time of peace, and that we may with impunity go back to the pun and haul for profits regardless of the results to the community. Such a condition does not produce strength, but weakness; not harmony, but discord.

In the struggle that arises under the above conditions, between an autocratic ownership and an autocratic labor party, the economic laws which produce strength are largely disregarded and the whole industrial and business system becomes infected with such feebleness that it is incapable of supporting our complicated system of modern civilization. This is exactly what is happening in Eastern Europe, where civilization is tottering due to the fact that the industrial and business system by which it was supported is no longer functioning properly. The production portion seems to have absolutely broken down, hence there is a shortage everywhere of the necessities of life. This failure is undoubtedly due to a combination of causes; but whatever the cause, the result is the same, for the violation of economic laws, whether through interest, ignorance, or indolence, will ultimately, to use the language of a distinguished economist, "blow the roof off our civilization just as surely as the violation of the laws of chemistry will produce an explosion in the laboratory."

We must avoid the possibility of this explosion at all hazards. If we would accomplish this result we must begin at once not only to make clear what the correct economic laws are, but to take such steps in conformity with them as will get the support of the community in general, and lessen the danger of following Europe into the chaos toward which she seems heading.

Those who believed the war could last only a few months based their opinion on the destruction of wealth it would cause. They had absolutely no conception of the tremendous speed with which this loss might be made good by the productive force or modern industry. They did not understand that the controlling factor in the war would ultimately become *productive capacity.*

When we entered the war, it was of course necessary to raise money, and through the persistent use of the slogan *Money will win the war,* our loans were promptly oversubscribed. Although we were able to raise all the money we needed, we had difficulty in transforming that money quickly into fighting power, for we made the fundamental error of considering that those who knew how to raise money, also knew how to transform it into food and clothing, weapons, and ships. The sudden ending of the war prevented us from realizing how great this error was. Even a superficial review of what took place during 1918, however, reveals the fact that our efforts at production were sadly in-effective. So true is this that some of those in authority not only discouraged all efforts to show comparison between their promises and their performances in such a manner that the public could understand, but they actually forbade such comparisons to be made.

There was, in Washington, at the beginning of the war, however, one man who understood the necessity for just this kind of record, which should be kept from day to day and should show our progress in the work we had to do. This man was Brigadier General William Crozier, Chief of Ordnance. Apparently alone among those in authority at that time, he recognized the important principle that *authority and' responsibility for performa1we must be centered in the some individual, and organized his department on that basis.* Before the breaking out of the war a simple chart system, which showed the comparison between promises and performances, had been established in the Frankford Arsenal. This system General Crozier began to, extend throughout the Ordnance Department as soon as we entered the war, and in order that he might at all times see how each of his subordinates was performing the work assigned to him. As the method was new, progress was necessarily slow, but before General Crozier was removed from his position as Chief of Ordnance, in December,

1917, a majority of the ,activities of the Ordnance Department were shown in chart form so clearly that progress, or *lack of progress,* could be seen at once. No other government department had at, that time so clear a picture of its problem and the progress being made in handling it.

The following incident will serve to show the results that had been produced by this policy. Late in November, 1917, Dean Herman Schneider of the University of Cincinnati, was called to the Ordnance Department to assist on the labor problem. Before deciding just how he would attack his problem, he naturally investigated the activities of the department as a whole, with the result that early in December, 1917, he wrote General C. B. Wheeler, under whom he was working, a letter from which the following is an extract:

"The number of men needed for the Ordnance Program should be ascertainable in the production sections of the several divisions of the Ordnance Department. Investigation so far (in three production sections) discloses that, except in isolated cases, a shortage of labor is not evident.

"Each production section has production and progress chart systems. These seem to vary in minor details only. Even without rigid standardization, the charts give a picture of the progress of the whole Ordnance Program including lags and the causes therefore. Combined in one office and kept to date they would show the requirements as to workers, as well as to materials, transportation, accessory machinery, and all of the other factors which make or break the program.

"With a plan of this sort the Ordnance Department would be in a position to state *at any time its immediate and probable future needs in men, materials, transportation, and equipment.*

"The other Departments of the War Department (and of other departments engaged in obtaining war material) can, through their Production Sections, do what the Ordnance Department can do, namely, assemble in central offices their production and progress charts through which they would know their immediate and probable future needs.

"Finally, these charts assembled in one clearing office would give the data necessary in order *to make the whole program of war production move with fair uniformity, without disastrous competition and with justice to the workers."*

This letter not only sets forth clearly what General Crozier had accomplished, but it shows still more clearly Dean Schneider's conception of the problem which at that time lay immediately before us. General Crozier's successors allowed the methods which had been developed to lapse, and Dean Schneider's vision of the industrial problem and ability to handle it were relegated to second place.

The methods referred to by Dean Schneider were afterward adopted in an elementary way by the Shipping Board and by the Emergency Fleet Corporation. Although they were never used to any great extent by those in highest authority, who apparently were much better satisfied simply to report what they had done, rather than to compare it too closely with what they might have done, they were used to great advantage by many who were responsible for results in detail.

Fig. 6 is a sample of the charts referred to above. This is an actual Ordnance Department chart, entered up to the end of December, 1917, the names of the items being replaced by letters. It was used to illustrate the methods employed and to instruct people in the work.

The distance between the current date and the end of the heavy or cumulative line indicates whether the deliveries of any article are ahead or behind the schedule and how much. It is thus seen that the short lines indicate instantly the articles which need attention.

Similar charts were used during the war to show the schedules and progress in building ships, shipyards, and flying boats-and are now being used for the same purpose in connection with the manufacture of many kinds of machinery. The great advantage of this type of chart, known as the straight line chart, is that it enables us to make a large number of comparisons at once.

As said before, when General Crozier was removed from his office about the 1st of December, 1917, he had a majority of the items for which he was responsible charted in this manner, and was rapidly getting the same kind of knowledge about the other items. Charts of this character were on his desk at all times, and he made constant use of them.

This chart is shown only as a sample and represents a principle. Each item on such a chart as the above may have been purchased from a dozen different suppliers, in which case the man responsible for procuring such articles had the schedule and progress of each contract charted in a manner similar to that on Chart 6. Chart 7 is such a chart. The lines on Chart - 6 represented a summary of all the lines on the corresponding detail charts.

Figure 6

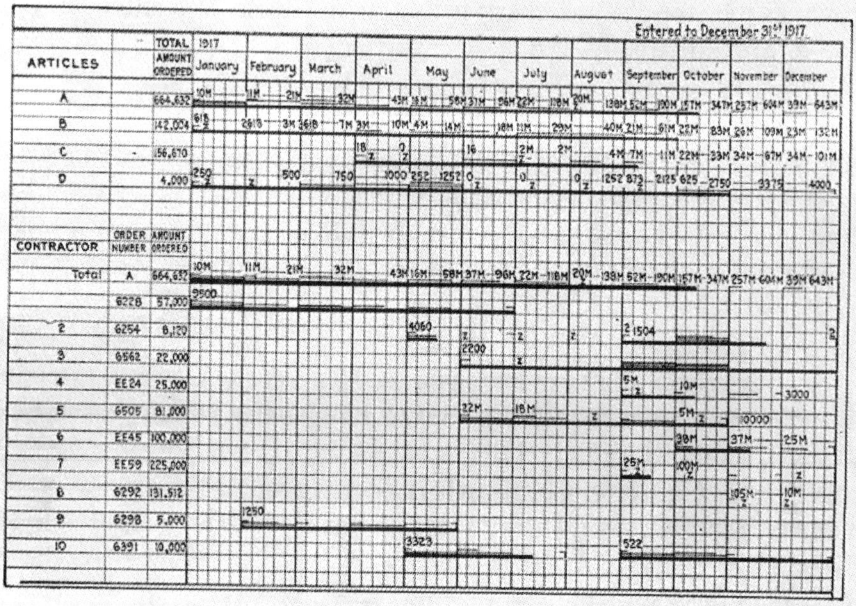

Fig. 6.—Progress Chart (top) and Fig. 7.—Order Chart (bottom)

At the left of the upper chart is a list of articles to be procured. The amounts for which orders have been placed are shown in the column headed "Amount ordered." The dates between which deliveries are to be made are shown by angles. The amount to be delivered each month is shown by a figure at the left side of the space assigned to that month. The figure at the right of each time space shows the total amount to be delivered up to that date.

If the amount due in any month is all received, a light line is drawn clear across the space representing that month. If only half the amount due is received, this line goes only half way across. In general, the length of the light line or the number of lines indicates the amount delivered during that month.

The heavy line shows cumulatively the amount delivered up to the date of the last entry. It will be noted that, if this line is drawn to the scale of the periods through which it passes, the distance from the end of the line to the current date will represent the amount of time deliveries are behind or ahead of the schedule. It is thus seen that the short cumulative lines are the ones which require attention, as they represent items that are farthest behind schedule. Z represents no deliveries. The top line on the lower chart is a summary of the individual orders and is represented on the upper chart by line A.

Similar charts were used during the war to show the schedules and progress in building ships, shipyards, and flying boats – and are now being used for the same purpose in connection with the manufacture of many kinds of machinery. The great advantage of this type of chart, known as the straight line chart, is that it enables us to make a large number of comparisons at once.

From the illustrations given the following principles upon which this chart system is founded are easily comprehended:

First: The fact that all activities can be measured by the amount of time needed to perform them.

Second: The space representing the time unit on the chart can be made to represent the amount of activity which should have taken place in that time.

Bearing in mind these two principles, the whole system is readily intelligible and affords a means of charting all kinds of activities, the common measure being time.

Note: There was no figure 7 in the original book.

Chapter 9 – DEMOCRACY IN THE SHOP

(Man Records)

IN the chapter on "An Extension of the Credit System," we referred only to financial credit. The term credit, of course, has a much broader meaning. For instance, when a man has proved his knowledge on a certain subject, we "give him credit" for that knowledge; when he has proved his ability to do things, we give him "credit" for that ability. In other words, we have confidence that he will make good. The credit which we give a man, or the confidence which we place in him, is usually based on record. We gave him credit for being able to handle the biggest job we had, and our faith was not misplaced. If we had an exact record of the doings of every man, we should have a very comprehensive guide for the placing of confidence and the extending of credit – even financial credit.

Inasmuch, however, as our record of individuals is exceedingly meager and our information concerning them is usually derived from interested parties, we have very little substantial basis for placing confidence in or extending credit to people in general. It is therefore hardly to be expected that a business system will risk investment without a: more substantial guarantee for the financial credit it extends. It would seem, then, that if we really wish to establish such a credit system as is described in Chapter VI, we must keep such a record of the activities of individuals as will furnish the information needed to give a proper guarantee.

All records, however, are comparative, and the record of a man's performance is comparatively valueless unless we are able to compare what he has done with what he should have done. The possibilities in the modern industrial system are so great that there is scarcely any conception of them by people in general. In fact, many accomplishments which have been heralded as quite extraordinary are shown on careful examination to have been quite the reverse, when a comparison is made with the possibilities.

In the past if a man has accomplished a desirable result, we have been pretty apt to let it go on its face value, and have seldom inquired into how it was done. We have no criticism of this as a habit of the past, but the war has brought an entirely different viewpoint into the world, and shown others besides Americans how inefficiently the world is conducting its civilization. Other peoples have realized that the real asset of a nation is its human power, and undoubtedly will soon begin to adopt means of measuring this power to the end that they may use it more effectively.

Some of us have made a start in this work by keeping individual records of operatives, showing-as nearly as possible what they have done in comparison with what they might have done, with the reasons for their failing to accomplish the full amount. By systematically attempting to remove the obstacles which stood in the way of complete accomplishment, we have secured a remarkable degree of co-operation, and developed in workmen possibilities which had been unsuspected. Further, we have developed the fact that nearly all workers welcome any assistance which may be given them by the foreman in removing the obstacles which confront them, and teaching them to become better workers. Chart No.8 is an actual chart of this type from a factory and covers a period of two weeks. Each working day was ten hours, except Saturday, which was five. The charts are ruled accordingly. If a worker did all that was expected of him in a day the thin line goes clear across the space representing that day, and if he did more or less, the number of such thin lines or the length of the line indicate the amount. The number of days' work he did in a week is represented by the heavy line. Where... ever a dotted line is shown, it indicates that during that time the man worked on a job for which we had no estimated time. The letters are symbols indicating the cause of failure to perform the full amount of work. A key to these symbols follows Chart No.8.

Inasmuch as, according to our idea of management, it is a foreman's function to remove the obstacles confronting the workmen, and to teach them how to do their work, an average of the performance of the workmen is a very fair measure of the efficiency of the foreman.

This is shown by the line at the top of the chart. It may readily be seen that such a chart system gives a very fair means of fixing the compensation of workers and foremen, and a series of such charts kept up week after week will give us a measure of the amount of confidence which we may place in the individual foreman and workman, for if all obstacles are removed by the foreman the workman's line is a measure of his effectiveness.

Just as the line representing the average of all the workers is a measure of the foreman, so a line representing the average of all the foremen is in some degree at least a measure of the superintendent.

The improvement which has been made by workers under our teaching and record-keeping systems involves more than is at first apparent. For instance, it has clearly been proven that poor workmen are much more apt to migrate than good workmen. The natural conclusion from this is that if we wish to make workmen permanent, our first step must be to make better workmen of them. Our experience proves this conclusion to be correct.

Many of our large industrial concerns have estimated that the cost of breaking in a new~ employee is very high-running from about $35.00 up. We have already satisfied ourselves that if only a fraction of this amount is expended in training the inferior workman, we can reduce migration very materially. In other words, money spent in proper teaching and training of workmen is a highly profitable' investment for any industrial concern, provided there is some means of measuring and recording the result. So beneficial have our training' methods proved that we are inclined to believe that *the practice of stealing good workmen from one's competitor will ultimately prove to be as unprofitable as stealing his property.*

Before the rise of modern industry the world was controlled largely by predatory nations who held their own by exploiting and taking by force of arms from their less powerful neighbors. With the rise of modern industrialism, productive capacity has been proven so much stronger than military power that we believe the last grand scale attempt to practice the latter method of attaining wealth or power has been made. In this Great War it was clearly proven that *not what we have* but *what we can do* is the more important. It clearly follows, then, that the workers we have are not as important as our ability to train others; again illustrating the fact that our productive capacity is more important than our possessions.

That the methods which I have here so inadequately described are of broad applicability has been proven by the fact that they have received enthusiastic support of the workmen wherever they have been tried. As previously said, it is undoubtedly true that the "efficiency" methods which have been so much in vogue for the past twenty years in this country, have failed to produce what was expected of them. The reason seems to be that we have to a large extent ignored the human factor and failed to take advantage of the ability and desire of the ordinary man to learn and to improve his position. Moreover, these "efficiency" methods have been applied in a manner that was highly autocratic. This alone would be sufficient to condemn them, even if they had been highly effective, which they have not.

In this connection it has been clearly proven that better results can be accomplished if the man who instructs the workman also inspects the work and 'not only shows the workman where he is wrong, but how to correct his errors, than if the inspection is left to a comparatively ignorant man, who is governed by rules. The attempt to combine instruction and inspection in one man has met with the highest approval among the workmen, with the result of better work and less loss. This method is contrary to the usual practice, inasmuch as instruction and inspection have been considered two functions, the former requiring an expert and the latter a much less capable, and hence cheaper, man. . We are satisfied that this analysis is defective; the inspector who can show the workman how to avoid his errors is usually worth far more than the extra compensation required to secure his services. It may be impossible to measure the exact material value of these methods individually, but the total effect is reflected in an improved and increased product at a lower cost.

Figure 8

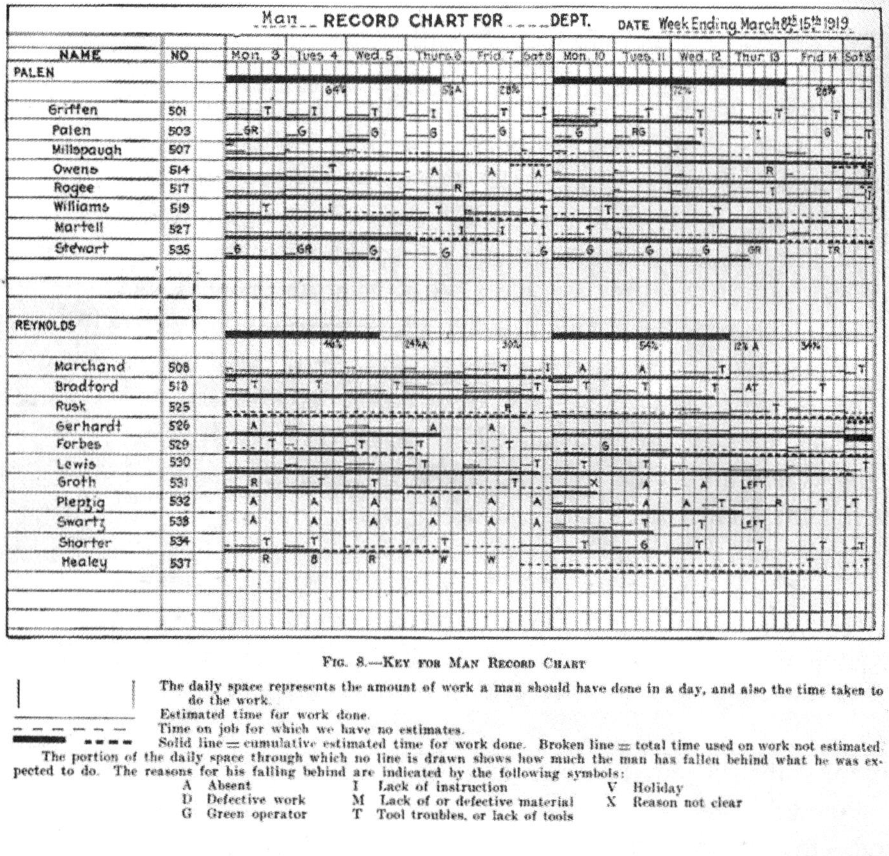

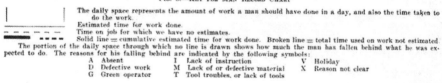

FIG. 8.—KEY FOR MAN RECORD CHART

The daily space represents the amount of work a man should have done in a day, and also the time taken to do the work.
Estimated time for work done.
Time on job for which we have no estimates.
Solid line = cumulative estimated time for work done. Broken line = total time used on work not estimated. The portion of the daily space through which no line is drawn shows how much the man has fallen behind what he was expected to do. The reasons for his falling behind are indicated by the following symbols:

A Absent   I Lack of instruction   V Holiday
D Defective work   M Lack of or defective material X Reason not clear
G Green operator   T Tool troubles, or lack of tools

Inasmuch as there is no necessity for any coercion in applying these methods when we have all, instructor who is capable of being a leader, we rapidly attain a high degree of democracy in the shop. On the other hand, if the instructor chosen fails to measure up to the standard of leadership, it is never long before his shortcomings are exposed, for through the medium of our charts available facts are easily comprehended by all. By these methods we automatically select as leader the man who knows what to do and how to do it, and when he has been found and installed, progress is rapid and sure.

Chapter 10 – DEMOCRACY IN MANAGEMENT

(Machine Records)

HAVING demonstrated by experience that it is possible to run a shop democratically and that the idea of giving every man a fair show and rewarding him accordingly is not really absurd, we naturally ask how far upward into the management we can carry this principle. The world still believes that authority must be conferred, and has a very faint conception of what we mean by *intrinsic authority,* or the authority that comes to a man who knows what to .do and how to do it, and who is not so much concerned with being followed as on getting ahead.

The problem of the manager is much wider than that of the superintendent or the foreman, for he must see that there is work to be done, materials to work with and men to do the work, besides numerous other things which are not within the sphere of the foreman.

The object of a shop being to produce goods, the first problem which comes to him is to find out to what extent the shop is performing the function for which it was built. In other words, are the various producing machines operating all the time and if not, why not? An opportunity for our chart comes in again, and the reason why a machine did not work at all is indicated by symbols. Chart No.9 is one of this type. The thin lines represent the number of hours each day a machine was operated; the heavy line represents the total number of hours it operated during the week. The symbols indicate the causes of idleness; some were due to lack of work; some to lack of material; some to lack of men; some on account of repairs, etc. If we have not worked enough to keep the shop busy, we must look for the cause by asking: Is there work to be had? Is our price low enough? Is our quality good enough? The answer to the first two must be determined by the manager in connection with the sales department. The third by the manager in connection with the shop superintendent. If our idleness is due to lack of material, the question must be taken up with the buyer and store-keeper. If it is due to lack of help, the labor policy and the wage system must be studied. If the idleness is due to repairs on machinery, the question is one for consideration by the superintendent and the maintenance department. In every case the responsibility for a condition is traced directly to its source. Moreover, as it is entirely possible to determine the expense incurred by idleness, such expense may be allocated directly to the responsible parties.

Inasmuch as a real management system is simply a mechanism for keeping all concerned fully advised as to the needs of a shop, and for showing continuously how these needs have been supplied, the *comparison between what each man from the top to the bottom did and what he should have done* is easily made. Under a system of management based on our charts, it soon becomes evident to all, who is performing his function properly and who is not. A man who is not making a success, knows about it as soon as anybody else, and has the opportunity of doing better if he can. If he is not making good, it is very seldom that he has any desire to hold on to the job and advertise his incompetence to his fellows. Moreover, it 'takes but a short experience with these methods to convince a man that his record will discredit him very much if he uses opinions instead of facts in determining his methods and policies. We are thus able to apply the same standards to those in authority that we apply to the workmen. In other words we ask of all-how well did he perform his task. A short line on a chart points unfailingly to him who needs most help.

Figure 9

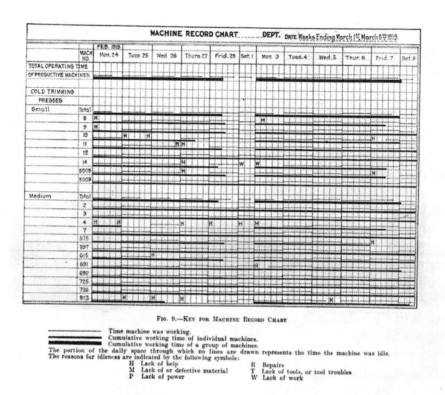

The Machine Record charts just referred to have to do with what proportion of the plant was operated. The Man Record charts indicate the effectiveness with which the machines were operated during the time they were operated. For instance, if a machine were operated only one-half the time, and with only one-half of its effectiveness during that time, we should get out of the machine only one quarter of its possible use. A combination, therefore, of these two sets of charts, which gives a measure of the manager, is a basis of our faith in him, and a measure of the financial credit that may be extended to him as a producer. A little consideration will show that such a record is a far safer basis for financial credit in many cases than physical property, and affords a means of financing ability or productive capacity as well as owners. It is not to be concluded that this subject is being presented in its final and complete form, but it is claimed that enough has been established to enable us to make, *an intelligent start in the operation of the new credit system, which the Federal Government was obliged to adopt without any guide.*

Further, it is safe to say that if such records as the ones just described had been available for the prominent business men of the country at the breaking out of the war, we should have been saved much time, and the expenditure of many millions of dollars.

The fact that such a system is applicable to the arts of peace as well as those of war; that it will pay for itself over and over again while it is being installed; and that it will enable us to value men according to service they can render, would seem to be sufficient reason why we should lose no more time than is necessary in taking steps to extend it throughout the nation. The fact that it is not an efficiency system as the term is generally understood, nor a system of scientific management as that term is understood, but simply one which enables us to use all the knowledge available and in a manner which is intelligible to the most ordinary workman as well as to the best educated executive, is responsible for the enthusiasm with which it has been received by the workmen as well as the executive. It is designed to enable an of us to use all the knowledge we have to the best advantage, and does not in the slightest interfere with, but rather supplements and supports, the work of those whose problem is to acquire additional knowledge.

In the preceding chapters we have given our view of the economic situation; of the forces that were affecting it, and whither it was tending. We have also shown our mechanism for making effective use of all the knowledge available. We also see that with increase in the amount and availability of knowledge the more certain our course of action is outlined, and the less we need to use opinion or judgment.

Moreover, our record charts invariably indicate the capable men, and not only give us an indication of how to choose our leaders, but a continual measure of the effectiveness of their leadership after they are chosen. We thus eliminate, to a large extent at least, opinion or judgment in the selection of leaders, and in so far do away with autocratic methods from whatever source.

Chapter Eleven – "THE RELIGION OF DEMOCRACY"

FOR over a thousand years the history of the world has been made by two great forces-the church and the state-the church basing its power on idealism and moral forces, the state depending almost entirely upon military power. At times these two forces have seemed for a while to cooperate, and then to become antagonistic. Today they are absolutely distinct, working in different fields, with but little ground in common, and a rival claims the middle of the stage, for during the last century there has come -into the world another force, which has concerned itself but little with our religious activities, and interested itself in our political activities only in so far as it could make the political forces serve its ends. I speak of the modern business system, based on the tremendously increased productive capacity of the race due to the advance of the arts and sciences. The rapid expansion of this new power has thrown all our economic mechanism out of gear, and because it failed to maintain a social purpose, which is common to both of the other forces, produces cross-currents and antagonisms in the community which are extremely detrimental to society as a whole.

One hundred years ago, each family-certainly each community-produced nearly everything needed for the simple life then led.

The village blacksmith and the local mill served the community, which existed substantially as a self-contained unit.

With the growth of the transportation system and grand scale production many of the functions of the local artizans were taken over by the factory, just as the flour mills of Minneapolis supplanted the local mills, which went out of existence.

In the same manner other large centralized industries by superior service drove out of existence small local industries. By reason of improved machinery and a better technology the centralized industries were able to render this superior service, at the same time securing large profits for themselves. Unfortunately for the country at large, those who later came into control of these industries did not see that the logical basis of their profits was service. When, therefore, the community as a whole had come to depend upon them exclusively, they realized their opportunity for larger profits still, and so changed, their methods as to give profits first place, oftentimes ignoring almost entirely the subject of service. It is this change of object in the business and industrial system, which took place about the close of the nineteenth century that is the source of much of the woe that has recently come upon the world. Unless the industrial and business system can rapidly recover a sense of service and grant it the first place, it is hard to see what the next few years may bring forth.

The great war through which we have just passed has done away with political autocracy, apparently forever, but it has done nothing whatever in this country to modify the autocratic methods of the business system, which is a law unto itself and which now accepts no definite social responsibility. This force is controlled by and operated in the interest of ownership, with, in many cases, but little consideration for the interests of those upon whose labor it depends, or for that of the community. We should not be surprised, therefore, that the workman who is most directly affected by this policy is demanding a larger part in the control of industry, especially as the war has taught him, in common with most of us, that the method of operating an industry is more important to the community than the particular ownership of that industry. The result of this knowledge is that the workers throughout the world are striving everywhere to seize the reins of power. Unfortunately for the world at large, these workers as a rule have no clearer conception of the social responsibility than those already in control. Moreover, having had no experience in operating grand scale industry and business, it is more than likely that their attempt to do so will result disastrously to the community. The industrial system as a whole is thus threatened with a change of control which we can scarcely contemplate with equanimity. We naturally ask if there is any possible relief from the confusion with which we are threatened. We think there is, but not by any of the methods generally advocated by "intellectuals" who are not closely in touch with the moving forces.

One class believes that the answer comes in government ownership and government control of industries. The experience of the world so far does not, however, give much encouragement along these lines, for in some quarters where public utilities have to a large extent been run by the government, it is frankly admitted, that the government is being run by the business system, which leaves us just where we were, *unless we can get a social purpose into that system,* in which case the need for government ownership would disappear. Is such a thing possible? Unless it can be shown that a business system which has a social purpose is distinctly more beneficial to those who control than one which has not a social purpose, I frankly confess that there does not seem to be any permanent answer in sight. On the other hand, if it can be shown conclusively that a business system operated by democratic methods (and the test of such a system is that it acts without coercion and offers each man the full reward of his labor) is more beneficial to those who lead than the present autocratic system, we have a basis on which to build a modern economic state, and one which we can establish without a revolution, or even a serious jar to our present industrial and business system. In fact, so far as I have been able to put into operation the methods I am advocating, we have very materially reduced the friction .and inequalities of the present methods much to the benefit of both employer and employee.

In 1908 I wrote a paper for the American Society of Mechanical Engineers, on "training workmen" in which I used the following ex-pression: "The general policy of the past has been to drive; but the era of force must give way to that of knowledge, and the policy of the future will be to teach and to lead, to the advantage of all concerned."

This sentiment met with much hearty support, but inasmuch as no mechanism had at that time come into general use for operating industry in that manner, the sentiment remained for most people simply a fine sentiment. At that time the organization of which I am the head had already made some advance in the technology of such a system of management, and since that time we have continued to develop our methods along the same lines, as shown in the previous chapters of the book.

Throughout this little book we have attempted to make clear that those *who know what to do and how to do it* can most profitably be employed in teaching and training others. In other words, that they can earn their greatest reward by rendering service to their fellows as well as to their employers. It has only been recently that we have been able to get owners and managers interested in this policy, for all the cost systems of the past have recorded such teachers as non-producers and hence an expense that should not be allowed. Now, however, with a proper cost-keeping system supplemented by a man-record chart system, we see that they are really our most effective producers.

We have attempted in this book to show an example of the mechanism by which we have put into operation our methods, and some of the results that have been obtained by them, the most important of which is that under such a system no "blind guides" can permanently hold positions of authority, and that leadership automatically gravitates to those who know what to do and how to do it. Moreover, we have yet to find a single place where these methods are not applicable, and where they have not produced better results than the old autocratic system. Moreover, they produce harmony between employer and employee and are welcomed by both. In other words, *we have proved in many places that the doctrine of service* which has been preached in the churches as religion is not only good economics and eminently practical, but because of the increased production of goods obtained by it, promises to lead us safely through the maze of confusion into which we seem to be headed, and to give us that industrial democracy which alone can afford a basis for industrial peace.

This doctrine has been preached in the churches for nearly two thousand years, and for a while it seemed as if the Catholic Church of the middle ages would make it the controlling factor in the world; but

146

the breaking up of the Church of the middle ages into sects, and the advance of that intellectualism which placed more importance upon words and dogma than upon deeds, gave a setback to the idea which has lasted for centuries. Now, when a great catastrophe has made us aware of the futility of such methods, we are beginning to realize that the present business system needs only the simple methods of the Salvation Army to restore it to health. It is absolutely sound at the bottom.

The attempt to run the world by words and phrases for the benefit of those who had the power to assemble those words and phrases involved us in a great war, and the continued application of these methods seems to be leading us into deeper and deeper economic confusion. We are therefore compelled to recognize that the methods of the past are no longer possible, and that the methods of the future must be simpler and more direct.

It should be perfectly evident that with the increasing complexity of the modern business system (on which modern civilization depends) successful operation can be attained only by following the lead of those who understand practically the controlling forces, and are willing to recognize their social responsibility in operating them.

Any attempt to operate the modern business system by people who do not understand the driving forces is sure to reduce its effectiveness, and any attempt to operate it in the interest of a class is not much longer possible.

For instance, under present conditions the attempt to drive the workman to do that which he does not understand results in failure, even if he is willing to be driven, which he no longer is; for he has learned that real democracy is something more than the privilege of expressing an opinion. We are thus forced into the new economic condition, and, whether we like it or not, will soon realize that only those *who know what to do and how to do it* will have a sufficient following to make their efforts worth while. In other words, the conditions under which the great industrial and business system must operate to keep our complicated system of modern civilization going successfully can be directed only by real leaders-men who understand the operation of the moving forces, and whose prime object is to render such service as the community needs.

In order to secure such leaders they must have full reward for the service they render. These rules out the dollar-a-year man, whose qualifications too often were not that he knew how to do the job, but that he was patriotic and could afford to give his services for nothing. In spite of such a crude way of selecting men to handle problems vital to the life of the nation, many did good work during the war.

The laws of the United States, however, forbid a man to work for the government for nothing, and both those who served at a dollar a year, and those who accepted that service, violated the spirit of the law, which was aimed to sustain the democratic practice of rewarding a man according to the service he rendered. Any other practice is undemocratic.

In 1847, Mr. Lincoln wrote: "To secure to each laborer the whole product of his labor, or as nearly as possible, is a worthy object of any good government. But then the question arises, how can a government best affect this? * * * Upon this the habits of our whole species fall into three great classes-useful labor, useless labor, and idleness. Of these, the first only is meritorious, and to it all the products of labor rightfully belong; but the two latter, while they exist, are heavy pensioners upon the first, robbing it of a large portion of its just rights. The only remedy for this is to, so far as possible, drive useless labor and idleness out of existence.

Attempts are always being made to eliminate the idleness of workmen and useless labor by the refusal of compensation. Unfortunately, however, there has been no organized attempt as yet to force capital to be useful by refusing compensation to idle capital, or to that expended uselessly. Capital which is expended in such a manner as to be non-productive, and capital which is not used, can receive interest only by obtaining the same from capital which was productive or from the efforts of workmen, in either of which cases it gets a reward which it did not earn, and which necessarily comes from capital or labor which did earn it.

Reward according to service rendered is the only foundation on which our industrial and business. System can permanently stand. It is a violation of this principle which has been made the occasion for socialism, communism, and Bolshevism. All we need to defeat these "isms" is to re-establish our industrial and business system firmly on the principles advocated by Abraham Lincoln in 1847, and we shall establish *an economic democracy that is stronger than any autocracy.*

Moreover, it conforms absolutely to the teachings of all the churches, for Christ, who was the first to understand the commanding power of service, thus stands revealed as the first great Economist, for economic democracy is simply applied Christianity. This was also clearly understood by the great leaders of the Church of the Middle Ages, whose failure to establish it as a general practice was largely due to the rise of an intellectualism which disdained practicality.

Now, however, when a great catastrophe has shown us the error of our ways, and convinced us that the world is controlled by deeds rather than words, we see the road to Universal Peace only through the change of Christianity from a weekly intellectual diversion to a daily practical reality.